Critical Encounters

RECOGNITIONS

detective/suspense · science fiction

Dick Riley, General Editor

CRITICAL ENCOUNTERS

Writers and Themes in Science Fiction

Edited by Dick Riley

FREDERICK UNGAR PUBLISHING CO. NEW YORK

Copyright © 1978 by Frederick Ungar Publishing Co., Inc.
Printed in the United States of America
Designed by Patrick Vitacco

Library of Congress Cataloging in Publication Data

Main entry under title:
Critical encounters.

   1. Science fiction, American—History and criticism—Addresses, essays, lectures. I. Riley, Dick.
PS374.S35C74   813'.0876   78–4300
ISBN 0–8044–2713–5
ISBN 0–8044–6732–3 pbk.

Contents

Editor's Foreword

This book of "critical encounters" in science fiction is intended for both the serious reader, looking for solid critical commentary, and for the fan who would like to know a little more about a favorite author or book. Science fiction offers to readers and writers alike enormous possibilities in locale and plot. It can create planets utterly different from our own, or show us parts of this one that might have been, or might still be. In it we find reflections of the human character in a wide range of societies and environments, human and nonhuman. *Critical Encounters* is an attempt to look a little more closely at several of these worlds.

Some of the most important names in science fiction are subjects for our essays—Bradbury, Clarke, Heinlein, Asimov, Le Guin, Herbert. Works that have become enduring classics or show the promise of doing so are treated—Herbert's *Dune*, Heinlein's *Stranger in a Strange Land*, Clarke's *Childhood's End*—as well as themes important to the genre in the past, such as robots and artificial intelligence in Asimov's seminal works. And there is a provocative examination of an issue that will no doubt play a large role in the genre in the future —the place of gender in human society, as exemplified thus far in feminist science fiction.

The essays included here—all written expressly for this volume—are notable not only for their careful thought, but also for their readable and largely informal style. They are not designed to disassemble the many worlds of science fiction, to analyze the life out of them. They aim rather to illuminate them, by exploring such aspects as the derivation of the water-saving rituals on arid Arrakis, the myths that operate on Le Guin's fictional planets, the impact that Heinlein's *Stranger* had on the counterculture of the Sixties. Notes can be found at the end of the book; to avoid the distraction of superscript numbers, all references are identified by page number and key words from the cited material.

At its best, science fiction has no peer in creating another universe of experience, in showing us what we look like in the mirror of technological society or through the eyes of a nonhuman. The essays here are offered as brief but lively guides to these worlds, making them perhaps more understandable, more accessible, and, it may be hoped, more real.

D. R.

1

Jean Fiedler and Jim Mele

ASIMOV'S ROBOTS

Although Isaac Asimov has written almost two hundred books, including mysteries, scientific texts, biblical studies, histories, and children's books, science fiction has given him his largest audience. And of all his creations, Asimov himself says, "If, in future years, I am to be remembered at all, it will be for (the) three laws of robotics."

These three laws, deceptively simple at first glance, have led to a body of work—twenty-two short stories, two novels, one novella—that has permanently changed the portrayal of robots in science fiction. Far from confining Asimov, these laws sparked his imagination, provoking unique and inventive speculation on a future technology and its effect on humanity.

Isaac Asimov was born on January 2, 1920, in Petrovichi, U.S.S.R., and was brought to the United States at the age of three. A brilliant student at Boys' High in Brooklyn, he went on, at the age of fifteen, to Columbia University, where he earned a B.S. in 1939, an M.A. in 1941, and finally a Ph.D. in biochemistry in 1948.

He began teaching at the Boston University School of Medicine in 1949 and in 1955 was appointed associate professor of biochemistry. By 1959 Asimov had given up teaching to concentrate entirely on writing.

Asimov sold his first science fiction story, "Marooned off Vesta," in 1938. Twenty-eight years later, his *Foundation* trilogy was voted the World Science Fiction Convention's prestigious Hugo award for the best all-time series, confirming his reputation as one of America's leading science fiction writers. He won a second Hugo as well as the Nebula award for *The Gods Themselves*, published in 1972.

As a reader of science fiction in the Thirties, Asimov says, he resented the Frankenstein concept then rampant—the mechanical man that ultimately destroys its master. Annoyed with what he saw as a purely Faustian interpretation of science, Asimov decided in 1940 to try his hand at writing stories about a new kind of robot, "machines designed by engineers, not pseudo men created by blasphemers."

"Robbie," his first robot story, unveils a machine with a "rational Brain," a machine created solely for the use of mankind and bound by three immutable laws that it cannot violate without destroying itself.

These laws, essential to Asimov's conception of the new robot, he dubbed the three laws of robotics: First law—a robot may not injure a human being or through inaction allow a human being to come to harm. Second law—a robot must obey the orders given it by human beings except when such orders would conflict with the first law. Third law—a robot must protect its own existence as long as such protection does not conflict with the first and second laws.

Despite their apparent simplicity, these laws are Asimov's most significant contribution to a new kind of science fiction. Using the three laws as the premise for all robotic action, he proceeded to write a series of stories and later two novels that presented the relationship of technology and humanity in a new light.

When "Robbie" first appeared in *Super Science Stories* in 1940, it is unlikely that any reader was able to discern the truly revolutionary nature of this elementary robot. "Robbie" is an uncomplicated, even naïve, story of a nonvocal robot who was built to be a nursemaid. From the beginning Asimov wages his own war on the Frankenstein image of the new robot. Gloria, the child, loves Robbie as a companion and playmate. Her mother, Grace, dislikes and distrusts the robot, whereas her father, George, acknowledges the three laws of robotics and sees the robot as a useful tool that can never harm his child.

Despite wooden characters and a predictable plot, this early robot story is the first step in Asimov's investigation of the potential inherent in the three laws and the as yet unforeseen ramifications of his new robotic premise.

In the stories that follow "Robbie," it seems obvious that Asimov's scientific background suggested a technique that he could use to investigate and exploit this new character, the non-Frankenstein robot. Like a scientist working in the controlled environment of a laboratory, Asimov took the three laws as an inviolable constant and logically manipulated them.

In a sense, the three laws *are* the plot in Asimov's early stories. By allowing the actions of the various robots seemingly to contradict one of the laws, Asimov creates a fictive tension, which he then releases by letting his human characters discover a logical explanation, one that works within the framework of the robotic laws.

Using this formula, Asimov followed "Robbie" with eleven more robot stories, all published in various science fiction pulp magazines, the best of which were collected under the title, *I, Robot*, and published by Gnome Press in 1950.

In the *I, Robot* stories, Asimov introduces three central human characters to link the stories together as well as a number of concepts that quickly become central to his expanding robotic world. Susan Calvin, a robot psychologist or roboticist, is the main character in some stories. She has an intuitive, almost uncanny understanding of the thought processes of Asimov's peculiar robots. When the stories leave the earth's surface, two new characters take over—Gregory Powell and Mike Donovan, trouble-shooters who field-test new robots. Susan Calvin remains behind to record their exploits for curious reporters and historians. All three are employees of U.S. Robots and Mechanical Men, the sole manufacturers of Asimovian robots.

By the second story in *I, Robot*, "Runaround," Asimov has invented a name for the phenomenon that sets his robots apart from all their predecessors—the positronic brain, a "brain of platinum-iridium sponge . . . (with) the 'brain paths' . . . marked out by the production and destruction of positrons." While Asimov has readily admitted, "I don't know how it's done," one fact quickly becomes clear; his positronic brain gives all of his robots a uniquely human cast.

In "Runaround" Powell and Donovan have been sent to Mercury to report on the advisability of reopening the Sunside Mining Station with robots. Trouble develops when Speedy (SPD-13), who has been designed specifically for Mercury's environs, is sent on a simple mission essential both to the success of the expedition and to their own survival.

Instead of heading straight for the designated target, a pool of selenium, Speedy begins to circle the pool, spouting lines from Gilbert and Sullivan, and challenging Powell and Donovan to a game of catch.

At first glance it seems that Speedy is drunk. However, never doubting that the three laws continue to govern the robot's behavior, as bizarre as it is, the two men proceed to test one hypothesis after another until ultimately they posit a theory that explains Speedy's ludicrous antics and "saves the day."

"Reason" presents the two engineers with an unexpectedly complex robot, the first one who has ever displayed curiosity about its own existence. Built to replace human executives on a distant space station, Cutie (QT-1), trusting his own intuitive feeling, comes to his own "logical" conception of a universe that does not include Earth, human creators, or anything beyond the space station.

Eventually Cutie arrives at the belief that the generator of the space station is "The Master," that he, QT-1, is his prophet, and that Donovan and Powell are inferior stopgap creations that preceded him.

Although in the end Asimov still uses the laws to explain Cutie's behavior, for the first time the robot is no longer merely a device to illustrate the workings of his three laws. It seems obvious that Asimov in his manipulation went a step further in the characterization of this robot. Cutie is not a simple tool; he is curious, intuitive, considerate of his "inferiors," Donovan and Powell, humoring their "misplaced notions," and ultimately but unconsciously fulfilling the requirements of the first robotic law—to protect human life.

When Asimov first began to write about robots, he knew what he did not want to perpetuate. Now with Cutie's creation, he began to see the real ramifications of robots who must obey the three laws. He knew that they were tremendous technological achievements, but now there has been an alteration in the technology; this new technology is softened by human moral and ethical qualities.

A robot unintentionally endowed with the ability to read minds is the hero of "Liar." Of course, this ability has profound effects on the robot's interpretation of the three laws, an interpretation so logical, so simple that it is overlooked by everyone, including the famed robot psychologist, Susan Calvin. Herbie (RB-34) not only reads minds, but he must consider human psychic well-being in all his actions.

Working within self-imposed limits often gives rise to the temptation to transgress those limits, if only briefly. In "Little Lost Rabbit," Asimov succumbs to the temptation of tampering with the first law. With his background in biblical studies, he inevitably finds that such a transgression of absolute law can only lead to disaster. He creates a robot who, while still forbidden to harm a human being, has no compulsion to prevent through inaction a human from coming to harm. This modification is performed only because of dire need and over the strenuous objections of the robotists. His forbidden apple tasted, Asimov is content to return to the invariable perimeter of his three laws in the rest of the stories.

By the time he gets to "Escape," Asimov has realized that the emotional characteristics of the robotic personality made possible by the injunctions of the three laws have become in unexpected ways the robot's greatest strength. In "Escape," the largest positronic brain ever built (so large it is housed in a room rather than in a humanoid body) is asked to solve a problem that has already destroyed a purely functional computer. Susan Calvin and the others realize that the problem of developing a hyperspace engine must involve some kind

of dilemma that the purely rational computer cannot overcome.

Endowed with the flexibility of a personality, even an elementary personality, the brain ultimately does solve the problem, but not without a curious humanlike reaction.

The nub of the problem is that hyperspace travel demands
that human life be suspended for a brief period, an unthinkable act expressly forbidden by the first law. The brain, although able to see beyond the temporary nature of the death,
is unbalanced by the conflict. Whereas a human might go on
a drunken binge, the brain escapes the pressure of his dilemma by seeking refuge in humor and becoming a practical
joker. He sends Powell and Donovan off in a spaceship without internal controls, stocked only with milk and beans, and
arranges an interesting diversion for the period of their temporary death.

"Evidence" presents a situation in which Stephen Byerley,
an unknown candidate, is running for public office, opposed
by political forces that accuse him of being a robot, a humanoid robot. The story unfolds logically, with the three laws
brought into play apparently to substantiate the opposition's
claim. Waiting for the proper dramatic moment, Byerley dis-
proves the charges by disobeying the first law. And ultimately,
in a climax worthy of O. Henry, Susan Calvin confronts Byerley, leaving the reader to wonder whether Byerley is really a
robot or a human being.

In a sense this is the most sophisticated story in *I, Robot*.
As a scientist accustomed to the sane and ordered world of
the laboratory, Asimov has had a tendency until now to tie
together all the loose strands. In "Evidence," he leaves his
reader guessing, and strangely, this looser, more subtle technique makes the story especially memorable.

The final story in the *I, Robot* collection, "The Evitable
Conflict," takes place in a world divided into Planetary Regions
and controlled by machines. In this story, the interpretation
of the first law takes on a dimension so broad that it can in
effect be considered almost a nullification of the edict: A
machine may not harm a human being. Susan Calvin is called

in by the World Coordinator—the same Stephen Byerley we have met in "Evidence"—to help determine why errors were occurring throughout the regions in the world's economy. Indications are that the machines, the result of complicated calculations involving the most complex positronic brain yet, had been working imperfectly. All four machines, one handling each of the Planetary Regions, are yielding imperfect results.

Calvin, with her intimate knowledge of robot psychology, discerns that the seeming difficulty is attributable to yet another interpretation of the first law. In this world of the future, the machines work not for any single human being but for all mankind, so that the first law becomes "No machine may harm *humanity* or through inaction allow *humanity* to come to harm."

Because economic dislocations would harm humanity and because destruction of the machines would cause economic dislocations, it is up to the machines to preserve themselves for the ultimate good of humanity even if a few individual malcontents are harmed.

Asimov seems to be saying through Susan Calvin that mankind has never really controlled its future. "It was always at the mercy of economic and sociological forces it did not understand—at the whims of climate and the fortunes of war. Now the machines understand them; and no one can stop them, since the machines will deal with them as they are dealing with the society—having as they do the greatest of weapons at their disposal, the absolute control of the economy."

In our time we have heard the slogan "The greatest good for the greatest number," and have seen sociopolitical systems of government that supposedly practice it. But men, not machines, have been in control. As Susan Calvin says, in the year 2052, "For all time, all conflicts are finally evitable. Only the machines from now on are inevitable."

Perhaps Asimov realized that, following his ever logical extensions of the three laws, he had gone the full robotic circle and returned his "new" robots to the Faustian mold. Although benign rulers, these machines were finally beyond their creators' control, a situation just as chilling as Frankenstein's monster destroying its creator.

Having foreseen the awesome possibility, Asimov leaves this machine-controlled world, to return to it only one more time, in 1974.

The *I, Robot* collection, one of two books published by Asimov in 1950, was an auspicious debut for a writer whose name would become one of the most widely recognized in contemporary science fiction. As well as reaching a new audience, *I, Robot* quickly became considered a classic, a standard against which all other robot tales are measured.

After *I, Robot,* Asimov wrote only one more short robot story—"Satisfaction Guaranteed"—before his first robot novel in 1953. The novel, called *The Caves of Steel,* was followed by five more short stories and in 1956 by the final, at least to date, robot novel, *The Naked Sun.*

The Rest of the Robots, including the six short stories and the two novels, as well as two early stories that predate the three laws, was issued by Doubleday in 1964. Although not truly the "rest" (Asimov has written at least five later stories), together with *I, Robot* it forms the major body of Asimov's robot fiction.

While the two novels in *The Rest of the Robots* represent the height of Asimov's robot creations, the quality of the short stories is quite uneven, and most seem to have been included only for the sake of historical interest. Three stories, however, "Satisfaction Guaranteed," "Risk," and "Galley Slave," do stand out.

Although not one of Asimov's most inventive stories, "Satisfaction Guaranteed" presents still another unexpected interpretation of the robotic laws.

Tony (TN-3) is a humanoid robot placed as an experiment in the home of Claire Belmont, an insecure, timid woman who feels she is hindering her husband's career. Under the aegis of Susan Calvin, U.S. Robots introduces Tony, designed to manage a normal household, into Claire's home, hoping that the success of this experiment will help ease the prevalent fear of robots and lead to their acceptance as household tools.

While Larry Belmont, Claire's husband, is out of town—a simple device on Asimov's part to leave Claire and the robot sequestered together—Claire experiences a variety of emotions ranging from fear to admiration and finally to something akin to love.

In the course of his household duties, Tony recognizes that Claire is suffering psychological harm through her own sense of inadequacy. Broadening the provision of the first law to include emotional harm, he makes love to her in a situation he contrives to strengthen her self-image.

Despite its lack of subtlety and polish, "Satisfaction Guaranteed" presents a loving, even tender robot that paves the way for Daneel Olivaw, the humanoid robot investigator in the novels.

In "Risk," an experimental spaceship with a robot at the controls is for some unknown reason not functioning as it was designed to do; a disaster of unknown proportions is imminent. Assembled scientists agree that someone or something must board the ship, find out what has gone wrong, and deactivate the ship's hyperdrive, Susan Calvin refuses, however, to send one of her positronic robots and instead suggests a human, engineer Gerald Black.

Not because of great physical danger, but because there is a frightening probability of brain damage, Black angrily refuses. Despite the danger that Black could return "no more than a hunk of meat who could make (only) crawling motions," Calvin contends that her million-dollar robots are too valuable to risk.

Threatened with court-martial and imprisonment on Mercury, Black finally boards the ship and discovers what went wrong. Returning a hero, Black is enraged that a human could be risked instead of a robot and vows to destroy Calvin and her robots by exposing to the universe the true story of Calvin's machinations.

With a neat twist displaying that Calvin's understanding of humans is as penetrating as her vision of robots, she reveals that she has manipulated Black as adroitly as she does her mechanical men.

Perhaps Asimov was beginning to fear that his readers had grown to accept robots as totally superior to humans, a condition that could only lead to a predictable and constricting science fiction milieu. In "Risk," through Susan Calvin, he reminds Black and all other myopic humans of the limits of robotic intelligence when compared to the boundless capacity of the human mind:

> "Robots have no ingenuity. Their minds are finite and can be calculated to the last decimal. That, in fact is my job.
> "Now if a robot is given an order, a *precise* order, he can follow it. If the order is not precise, he cannot correct his own mistake without further orders. . . . 'Find out what's wrong' is not an order you can give to a robot; only to a man. The human brain, so far at least, is beyond calculation."

Foreshadowing the two novels, "Galley Slave," the last short story in *The Rest of the Robots*, shows an Asimov grown wary of overreliance on robotic labor.

Easy (EZ-27), a robot designed to perform the mental drudgery that writers and scholars must endure when preparing manuscripts for the printer, is rented by a university to free professors from proofreading galleys and page proofs.

Easy performs his duties perfectly until he makes a number of subtle changes in a sociology text written, strangely enough, by the one faculty member opposed to robots.

The changes, undetected until the text has been printed and distributed, destroy the author's career, and the result is a $750,000 suit against U.S. Robots. Susan Calvin, as always, is certain that the errors are the result of human meddling and not robotic malfunction.

In every other case, Asimov has chided shortsighted people for refusing to allow robots to free them from menial work. Now as a writer with technology encroaching on his own domain, Asimov's characterization of the antirobot argument is much more sympathetic than ever before.

Explaining his motives to Susan Calvin, the person responsible for Easy's misuse says,

"For two hundred and fifty years, the machine has been re-placing Man and destroying the handcraftsman. . . . A book should take shape in the hands of the writer. One must actu-ally see the chapters grow and develop. One must work and rework and watch the changes take place beyond the original concept even. There is taking the galleys in hand and seeing how the sentences look in print and molding them again. There are a hundred contacts between a man and his work at every stage of the game—and the contact itself is pleasurable and repays a man for the work he puts into his creation more than anything else could. *Your robot would take all that away.*"

By 1952 Asimov had written "three or four novels," all non-robotic. But in the course of discussing a possible new novel with Horace Gold, his editor at *Galaxy,* Asimov balked when "some sort of robotic plot" was suggested, and objected even more strenuously when his editor mentioned a robot detec-tive. "How," he asked, "can you be fair with the reader, if you can at will drag in futuristic devices?" When Gold re-sponded with, "What do you want . . . something easy?" Asi-mov said he had no choice but to get to work. He accepted the challenge of putting together two mass fiction hybrids and accomplished a fully developed work, *The Caves of Steel,* that does not violate the spirit of either.

Never one to retire good characters prematurely, Asimov published a second science fiction mystery, *The Naked Sun,* in 1956, reuniting human detective Elijah Baley and his robot partner Daneel Olivaw.

Asimov's basic theme in his short stories—an emotional ar-gument for technology as a useful, practical tool that cannot succeed without human direction—develops new subtlety and strength in the full-length novel *The Caves of Steel.* Here too, Asimov again uses the three laws of robotics as the premise for all plot action, a technique he perfected in his *I, Robot* stories and one well suited to the deductive reasoning essen-tial to murder mysteries.

Set two thousand years in the future, *The Caves of Steel* presents contrasting pictures of Earth and the Outer Worlds—

colonized planets throughout the Galaxy. Although the inhabitants of the Outer Worlds trace their origins to Earth, they are separated from it by much more than mere distance, now calling themselves Spacers and ruling the decaying mother planet as benevolent despots. Earth, as antitechnology as it can afford to be, has developed a fragile society torn apart by rioting and dissension. In contrast, the Outer Worlds' total reliance on technology, especially robots, has created stable but stagnant societies peopled by strong individuals with equally strong materialistic appetites.

On Elijah Baley's Earth eight billion people live in eight hundred Cities, "Each City . . . a semiautonomous unit, economically all but self-sufficient. It could roof itself in, gird itself about, burrow itself under. It became a steel cave, a tremendous self-contained cave of steel and concrete."

The close quarters as well as strained food and energy production systems have produced a communal though stratified society, which adopts a name first coined in the French Revolution—civism. People eat in common kitchens, utilize communal bathrooms called personals, watch communal television. Privileges ranging from a seat on the expressways to a private office with a window separate the various strata of the society, strata patterned after present-day civil service ranks.

Elijah Baley, a plainclothesman in the New York City police force, has reached the C-5 level, entitling him to a seat on the expressways during nonrush hours, a railing around his desk at work, a three-room apartment with a private wash basin, and three meals a week in his own kitchen with his wife Jessie and their son.

This secure little world is shaken when Baley is asked to investigate the murder of a Spacer scientist, a member of that elite Outer World compound on Earth called Spacetown.

Not only does the murder of a Spacer by an Earthman present grave danger of retribution to the vulnerable Earth, but Baley is forced to take on as a partner a Spacer robot, R. Daneel Olivaw. Since most humans on earth are as violently antirobot as they are anti-Spacer, Baley views this assignment with distaste, but is forced to accept it.

Until Asimov approaches the novel, his robot characters are developed at the expense of their flesh-and-blood counterparts. Traditionally, science fiction and to a lesser extent mystery writing have been long on story and short on characterization, and Asimov, except for a few memorable robots in the short stories, follows in the tradition. When he sets himself the problem of this new form, the mystery science fiction novel, however, his priorities, of necessity, shift, and Baley becomes his first rounded and developed human character. At the same time, Asimov's main robot character gains a new depth when teamed up with a dimensional human partner.

Despite thin secondary characters, Asimov's storytelling technique is so compelling that it more than compensates for any flaws. This storytelling faculty is further enhanced by his ability to illustrate convincingly his belief in a humanistic technology, typified by positronic robots, without disrupting his narrative with sermons.

Freed from the confining boundaries of the short story, Asimov's descriptive style also improves in both technique and drama. The science fiction writer must create a vision of worlds that do not exist. In *The Caves of Steel*, Asimov's inner vision of a future Earth is so clear that his descriptions are vivid, tight, and evocative without his resorting to tortured metaphor or superfluous adjectives.

His introduction to the City, for example, is a well-crafted combination of simile and carefully chosen sensory details:

> There were the infinite lights; the luminous walls and ceilings that seemed to drip cool, even phosphorescence; the flashing advertisements screaming for attention; the harsh steady gleam of the "lightworms" that directed THIS WAY TO JERSEY SECTIONS. FOLLOW ARROWS TO EAST RIVER SHUTTLE, UPPER LEVEL FOR ALL WAYS TO LONG ISLAND SECTIONS.
> Most of all there was the noise that was inseparable from

life: the sound of millions talking, laughing, coughing, calling, humming, breathing.

No directions anywhere to Spacetown, thought Baley.

He stepped from strip to strip with the ease of a lifetime's
practice. Children learned to "hop the strips" as soon as they
learned to walk. Baley scarcely felt the jerk of acceleration as
his velocity increased with each step. He was not even aware
that he leaned forward against the force. In thirty seconds he
had reached the final sixty-mile-an-hour strip and could step
aboard the railed and glassed-in moving platform that was the
expressway.

Vastly improved too is his dialogue. Asimov has mastered
the translation of speech into its written equivalent; but to
re-create the speech of a human being is a problem every nov-
elist faces. Credible robotic speech is a much less common
challenge, and in *The Caves of Steel* Asimov has developed a
form a dialogue for Daneel that is completely believable. Daneel's speech, while possessing the rather formal lilt one might
expect from a machine, also possesses a gentle, tempered
quality that allows him to pass for human. Though the reader
is always conscious of a slight mechanical flavor, it is quite
believable that no uninformed human being would ever suspect Daneel is anything but human. Even Daneel's name, the
result, Asimov says, of a typographical error, mirrors his
slightly skewed human speech.

What made it possible for Asimov to extend his robot stories
to this novel length was the mystery element. He was able
to blend mystery and science fiction, something he was skeptical of accomplishing since it had never been done before,
because his three laws of robotics give the reader an absolute
framework for judging actions and motives.

The universality of the laws allows Baley to consider various
hypotheses in a future world without an unfair advantage
over the twentieth-century reader. When Baley considers the
possibilities that robots were involved in the murder, arm-
chair detectives can draw their own conclusions.

In turn, this longer form allows Asimov to exploit fully his argument: If humanity is to survive, it must overcome its fear of technology and learn to become its master.

The start of the novel finds Baley the typical Earthman, wary of robots, distrusting them, needing frequently to re-establish his superiority over them. The longer he works with Daneel, the better he comes to understand the real implications of robot technology and the dire consequences if Earth stubbornly continues to reject that technology.

As the novel draws to an end, Baley expresses an almost missionary zeal in his attempt to pass on to the antirobot forces what he has learned:

> "What are we afraid of in robots? If you want my guess, it's a sense of inferiority. . . . They seem better than us—only they're *not*. That's the damned irony of it."
>
> Baley felt his blood heating as he spoke. "Look at this Daneel I've been with for over two days. He's taller than I am, stronger, handsomer. . . . He's got a better memory and knows more facts. He doesn't have to sleep or eat. He's not troubled by sickness or panic or love or guilt.
>
> "But he's a machine. I can do anything I want to him, the way I can to that microbalance right there. . . .
>
> "We can't ever build a robot that will be even as good as a human being in anything that counts, let alone better. We can't create a robot with a sense of beauty or a sense of ethics or a sense of religion. There's no way we can raise a positronic brain one inch above the level of perfect materialism.
>
> "We can't, damn it, we can't. Not as long as we don't understand what makes our own brains tick. Not as long as things exist that science can't measure. What *is* beauty, or goodness, or art, or love, or God? We're forever teetering on the brink of the unknowable, and trying to understand what can't be understood. It's what makes us men."

It is a persuasive argument, one that Asimov carefully highlights in his logical evolution of a robot-based technology in the year 4000. This close attention to the future technology as well as to the formulation of an equally logical mystery may account for some flaws in his creation of a future society.

Increased population in the forty-first century has created social and economic pressures that have led to such devices as communal kitchens and bathrooms in crowded caves of steel. It seems probable that the atomic family would not have survived in this climate. Yet Elijah Baley is married, in the twentieth-century connotation of the word, to Jessie, and together with their son they live a normal nuclear family life; Baley works, Jessie keeps house, Bentley goes to school, and they all live together in their three-room apartment.

Asimov predicts radical changes in the hardware of human life. Yet he did not consider the possibility of a human revolution that was only a decade away. Jessie is a 1940-vintage domestic woman, as are her women friends; only white people are visible on this earth.

In the final analysis, however, *The Caves of Steel* easily rises above its shortcomings. Elijah Baley and Daneel Olivaw develop a unique relationship that sustains both the mystery plot and the science fiction premise, a relationship so intriguing and with so much vitality that it is a natural for a sequel.

And so when *The Naked Sun* was released in 1956 an eager audience awaited the Baley/Daneel reunion. Baley himself was hardly displeased at the resumption of their partnership, in sharp contrast to his original objections in *The Caves of Steel*.

Baley has been sent to Solaria, one of the Outer Worlds, to investigate a murder. This is a highly unusual event in the forty-first century—no Earthman has ever been allowed to visit the Outer Worlds and Earth's leaders suspect galactic intrigue.

Solaria is a large planet inhabited by only 20,000 people, a wealthy planet virtually without crime and without a police force. Baley, recommended by the Spacers he worked with in *The Caves of Steel*, panics even at the idea of leaving his City, let alone traveling in space to a distant planet. Agoraphobia is a malady common to all inhabitants of Earth and its closed Cities. Only Earth's dire political situation as the weakest member of the Galaxy and its desperate need for first-hand information about the Outer Worlds provide the leverage that pushes Baley aboard the Spacers' hyperspace craft.

As the spaceship lands on Solaria, Baley is losing the battle against his open-space phobia and waits uneasily for an unnamed Spacer partner. When Daneel walked in, "he had an almost unbearable desire to rush to the Spacer and embrace him, to hug him wildly, and laugh and pound his back and do all the foolish things old friends did when meeting once again after a separation."

Baley quickly finds that this Outer World is the exact opposite of Earth—eight billion Earthlings live in crowded dense Cities while Solarians live on 10,000-acre estates and find even the physical presence of a mate repugnant. With 10,000 robots for every human on the planet, Solaria possesses the most advanced robot economy in the universe, and Solarians all belong to a leisure class supported by two hundred million laboring robots. To Baley, it seems that "an observer from without might think Solaria a world of robots all together and fail to notice the thin human leaven."

Solaria's problems too are the exact opposite of those plaguing Earth. In *The Caves of Steel*, Earth is depicted on the verge of total destruction because of its antipathy to robots, that is, to modern technology. Solaria is faced with a destruction not as immediate but just as certain, as humans abrogate almost all responsibility by accepting the unquestioned supremacy of technology.

Echoing this prediction on a narrower, more personal level, *The Naked Sun* also shows that no matter how benign the technology and no matter what the internal safeguards, it will be used for illicit purposes by some. Technology is an ambiguous blessing, no matter who or what controls it.

This is a perception Asimov seemed to gain as he considered and described in writing the many undesirable permutations of robotic action possible within the constrictions of the three laws. There are sixteen years between "Robbie" and *The Naked Sun*. While the essential character of robots has not changed drastically, compare the world of Robbie to Solaria. Even if there were two hundred million nursemaids like Robbie, Asimov would never have portrayed this as a detriment to society.

In 1940, Asimov's blind faith in technology as a cure-all

mirrored a national religious fervor. After sixteen years of writing about robots, Asimov, although far from disenchanted, was admitting that technological development had serious dangers.

An important murder investigation is forcefully taken out of the hands of Solarian officials by Elijah Baley. Despite his feelings of inadequacy—Spacers have long been considered the superior beings of the Galaxy—Plainclothesman Baley is a natural leader on this planet largely because he comes from a world that has refused to accept the axiom "A robot can do it better." Even Daneel, who shared the spotlight with Baley in *The Caves of Steel*, is now eclipsed.

Furthermore, as representative of the human ethic, Baley commands more of Asimov's attention than in the earlier novel. He shows us the interior Baley, exploring and probing his phobias, his desires largely unexpressed until now, his internal strengths. Even his superiority over Daneel is more pronounced. Convinced that Daneel is merely an exceedingly useful tool, Baley no longer needs to twit him about only being a robot and even experiences twinges of guilt rather than a sense of accomplishment at having bested a robot when he has Daneel imprisoned. In fact, he is now more assured in his dealings with all robots, able to use or not use them as reason dictates.

Concurrently, robots are so well integrated into Asimov's own mythology that they no longer command the reader's attention as a novelty. Unencumbered by the pressures of stardom, Daneel has been freed to illustrate an exemplary robotic nature, a nature that highlights the positive aspects of advanced technology.

Not only have Baley and Daneel evolved for the better, Asimov has grown more adept in his other characterizations.

While his female characters Gladia Delmarre and Klorissa Cantoro are still cast in stereotype "feminine" molds, Asimov displays much more interest in endowing both with individual personality traits for the sake of lending depth to the characters. In obvious contrast, all of Jessie's actions and motives are directly related to plot in *The Caves of Steel*.

Gladia, wife of the murdered man and prime suspect, is a sensuous woman, the temptress who is plagued by her "nature." In her scenes with Baley, there is a strong sense of human interaction, each curious about the other, each probing with cautious discretion. The differences between their home planets Earth and Solaria are so great, and yet from the beginning their mutual sympathy is tangible to the reader.

Asimov, in an apparent decision to add sexual drives to Baley's growing character, succeeds in imparting an emotional reality well beyond mere desire to this intellectually conceived science fiction world.

The murdered man's assistant, Klorissa, seems at first glance to be a reincarnation of Susan Calvin, the cold, efficient, superior female scientist. But she too quickly rises above the stereotype as she exhibits nuances inherent in dimensional characterization—her aggressiveness is marred by doubt; personal inhibition occasionally disturbs her professional objectivity.

This skill and perception extends itself to a sizeable number of other minor characters, allowing Asimov to advance the story smoothly without dispelling his new-found balance between emotion and intellect.

The Naked Sun differs from *The Caves of Steel* in another important respect. Although still fueling the action, the mystery is not nearly as important as Asimov's speculations and conclusions about the future. *The Caves of Steel* is a good mystery set in a believable science fiction world. In *The Naked Sun*, however, the mystery takes a back seat as Asimov places stronger emphasis on the science fiction novel and all the broad connotations implicit in that genre.

This speculation on the evolution of man and his technology is carefully woven into the tapestry of the entire novel, but not until the end does Asimov reveal his overall design. Not until the very end of the novel does Asimov justify the immediate intuitive bond between Baley and Gladia.

Back on Earth, the murder solved, Baley finally comes to understand that Earth is "Solaria inside out." Solaria has embraced technology, excluding humanity; Earth has worshipped humanity, vilifying technology. Both seemed doomed to eventual extinction.

But Gladia's decision to leave Solaria for a new world and her "courage to face disruption of habits so deeply settled . . . seemed symbolic" to Baley. "It seemed to open the gates of salvation for *us* . . . for all mankind."

Comprehending the symbolic nature of her act, Baley realizes that he too has taken the first steps toward a new world. He "had left the City and could not re-enter. The City was no longer his; the Caves of Steel were alien. This had to be. And it would be so for others and Earth would be born again and reach outward."

Asimov has not lost his basic optimism that technology, used judiciously, is the key to the future. As he says in the epilogue to *The Naked Sun:*

> While I was writing *The Naked Sun,* it became perfectly clear to me that what I was working on was the second novel of a trilogy.
>
> In *The Caves of Steel* I had a society heavily overweighted in favor of humanity. In *The Naked Sun,* on the other hand, I had an almost pure robot society with only a thin leaven of humanity barely holding it together.
>
> What I needed to do next was form the perfect topper to my vision of the future by setting the third novel of the trilogy in Aurora, and depicting the complete fusion of man and robot into a society that was more than both and better than either.

The third novel—this *dernier mot* on robots—was actually begun in 1958, but unfortunately, "somewhere in the fourth chapter, between one page and the next, something happened. . . ."

Certainly Asimov did not stop writing, but he took off on a nonfiction binge, dictating such books as *The Genetic Code, Realm of Numbers, Words in Genesis, A Short History of Chemistry, The Neutrino,* and many, many others.

Although to date Asimov has not completed this third novel, the Baley/Daneel team is so popular with science fiction readers that in 1972 he sought to appease them with the short story "Mirror Image." More an exercise in reason and logic than a real story, the partners solve the mystery without even leaving Baley's New York City office.

Three years earlier he had resurrected his favorite character from the early robot tales—Susan Calvin. Setting out to write about a female robot in "Feminine Intuition," it was natural that he recall Calvin from retirement. Nearly eighty years old, she has not mellowed; her tongue is as sharp as ever, her patience as short. Of course, her penetrating judgment quickly solves the dilemma.

When *The Bicentennial Man and Other Stories* was published in 1975, it included, besides "Feminine Intuition," three other robot stories and a novella, as well as a miscellaneous collection of nonrobotic narratives. The three stories—"That Thou Art Mindful of Him," "The Life and Times of Multivac," and "The Tercentenary Incident"—echo "Evidence" and "The Evitable Conflict," the two final stories in *I, Robot*. While "That Thou Art Mindful of Him" and "The Life and Times of Multivac" are mildly interesting tales of Big Brother technologies, "The Tercentenary Incident," a reworking of the robot-passing-for-human theme, is not as effective as "Evidence."

Asimov's past robot stories and novels presupposed an historical context; each new story added to the growing body of robotic lore, serving as a foundation for what was to follow. In the novella "The Bicentennial Man," however, Asimov chose a subject incompatible with the constraints of this history. And so, exercising the fiction writer's prerogative, he eliminated what he no longer found useful. The result is a parallel world that still admits the inviolable nature of the three laws, carries over the names Susan Calvin and U.S. Robots, but discards all other historical precedents.

In past stories, Asimov was concerned with man's reaction to robots. "The Bicentennial Man" is the story of one robot's reaction to humanity—Andrew Martin's metamorphosis over the course of two hundred years into a man.

In this version of Earth, man's antipathy to robots has been replaced by wary tolerance; highly specialized robots are widely employed on an Earth possessing a stable robot/human economy and population.

Told from Andrew Martin's viewpoint, this is the first story in which Asimov has used a robot to narrate its own story, and ironically, Andrew Martin is Asimov's most consistently human character. His story is neither a mystery nor a generalized statement on mankind's future; it is the moving account of one being's struggle to realize his potential.

The last of Asimov's robot stories, at least to date, it stands as one of his best. It makes one wish all the more for that third novel.

2

Wayne L. Johnson

THE INVASION STORIES OF RAY BRADBURY

Seven-year-old Mink bursts into the house and begins snatching up kitchen utensils and apparently random bits of junk to be hauled outside for use in some mysterious game. "What's the name of the game?" inquires her mother. "Invasion!" the girl replies. Mink's mother goes on about her housework unaware that her daughter is telling the literal truth, and that what appears to be an innocent children's game is actually the prelude to an invasion of Earth by creatures from another world—Ray Bradbury style.

The theme of invasion is one of the oldest in science fiction. The early idea that other planets might be inhabited quite naturally suggested the possibility of eventual contact between our world and another. If the theory of evolution were correct, then it was conceivable that life forms on other planets had begun evolving thousands, even millions of years before those on Earth. Intelligent beings on Mars, for instance, might already be technologically advanced enough to visit Earth. Should they decide to do so, wouldn't their very advancement prove a threat to us?

H. G. Wells's book *The War of the Worlds* (1898) answered the question with a very dramatic yes. Wells's Martians— cold, emotionless, octopuslike horrors—fled their own dying planet and sought to conquer Earth, exterminating most of the human race in the process. The elements of the story were classic, and formed the basis for countless Earth vs.

Alien tales. Science fiction pulp magazines entered a phase of greatly increased popularity during the first half of the twentieth century. The two World Wars, with their immense firepower and destructiveness, created an atmosphere quite sympathetic to stories of interplanetary invasion and warfare. In America, Orson Welles's 1938 documentary-style radio version of *The War of the Worlds* was so realistic it caused a panic, and brought the idea of interplanetary invasion to general public consciousness.

Because of the dramatic possibilities of the subject, invasion became a popular theme in science fiction film and television productions. For instance, when Bradbury's short story "The Fog Horn" was made into a film, it was drastically altered to include an invasion motif. Thus Bradbury's rather touching story of a lonely ocean-dwelling dinosaur who mistakes a lighthouse foghorn for the cry of a long-lost mate became "The Beast from 20,000 Fathoms," in which a typical Hollywood monster charges ashore and demolishes large sections of New York City.

Bradbury has written a number of real invasion stories, of course, and these fall into two main groups: those that involve the invasion of Earth by aliens, and those that involve the invasion of Mars by Earthmen. The story about Mink and her mother belongs in the first group. It's called "Zero Hour," and comes from the collection of Bradbury's stories entitled *The Illustrated Man.* "Zero Hour" is essentially a suspense story. Mink's mother, Mrs. Morris, watches her daughter and the other young children in the neighborhood as they dart about playing their little game. As the day progresses, the game takes on some disturbing overtones. Mink and her friends appear to be talking to an unseen playmate in the rose bush, whom they address as Drill. When Mrs. Morris questions her daughter about this, the girl freely admits that Drill is an alien being from another dimension who is telepathically instructing the children. The aliens are teaching the children to build machines that will allow them to break through from their dimension into ours. The aliens know that no adult will take the children's game seriously until it is too late. This, of course, includes Mrs. Morris. Mink complains that some of the older boys have been teasing her and her friends: "They're so snooty, 'cause they're growing up. You'd think they'd know better. They were little only a coupla years ago. I hate them worst. We'll kill them *first*." To this Mrs. Morris is mildly patronizing. Half jokingly she asks if parents are to be killed too. Without hesitation, Mink answers that they are: "Drill says you're dangerous. Know why? 'Cause you don't believe in Martians. They're going to let *us* run the world. Well, not just us, but kids over in the next block too. I might be queen."

Our realization that Mink means business comes early in the story. We wait to see how long it will take Mrs. Morris to catch on, but we know the mother is essentially a helpless figure. What Mink says about her and other adults is true. Even if Mrs. Morris could accept her daughter's story, we know she would not be able to convince other adults. In any case, the idea is just too fantastic. At five o'clock, the previously announced "zero hour," Mr. Morris arrives home from work. Suddenly there is a loud buzzing outside, followed by explosions. Mrs. Morris realizes the truth. She drags her astonished husband up into the attic and locks the door. Heavy footsteps mount the stairs, the lock on the attic door melts and the door swings open. A smiling Mink peers in, tall blue shadows visible behind her, and ends the story by saying "Peekaboo."

"Zero Hour" derives much of its impact from its quiet suburban setting. Mrs. Morris's life is calm, well-ordered, secure. There is considerable irony in the fact that it is not the child's imagination that dominates the scene, but rather Mrs. Morris's fantasy of her own secure suburban life. This fantasy is so strong that the mother weaves all of her daughter's increasingly threatening remarks into it. Mink is only playing a game as all children do—isn't that reassuring? Mink, on the other hand, is not imagining things at all. She sees the facts quite clearly and, at least as far as Drill allows her to, she sees through her mother's illusions.

Aliens take advantage of a quiet suburban setting again in

"Boys! Raise Giant Mushrooms in *Your* Cellar!" from the collection *The Machineries of Joy.* This time the protagonist is one Hugh Fortnum. Fortnum looks out his window one bright Saturday morning and notices his next door neighbor, Mrs. Goodbody, spraying great clouds of insecticide in all directions. He asks her what the trouble is.

"What would you say," she asks, "if I told you I was the first line of defense concerning flying saucers?"

Fortnum humors her. "Fine . . . There'll be rockets between the worlds any year now."

" 'There already *are!*' She pumped, aiming the spray under the hedge. 'There! Take that!' "

A few minutes later, a special delivery package arrives for Fortnum's son Tom. Inspired by an ad in *Popular Mechanics,* Tom had sent away for a box of "Sylvan Glade Jumbo-Giant Guaranteed Growth Raise-Them-in-Your-Cellar-for-Big-Profit Mushrooms." Almost immediately, Tom disappears down into the cellar to begin raising his crop. In a plot essentially the same as "Zero Hour," it is Hugh Fortnum's fate to have an invasion plot unfold before his eyes while we wait to see if he will put the pieces of the puzzle together in time. The development of the story is more diffuse than in "Zero Hour," because, for one thing, Fortnum is not alone in uncovering the invasion. There is Mrs. Goodbody—though she does not seem aware of events outside her own garden—and there is Roger Willis. Willis flags down Fortnum later in the morning when Fortnum is driving to the store. Once in the car, Willis immediately begins complaining of an unexplainable feeling he has that "something's wrong with the world." Willis has no hard evidence to pin his anxiety on: "Maybe there's something wrong with the way the wind blows these weeds there in the lot. Maybe it's the sun up on those telephone wires or the cicadas singing in the elm trees. If only we could stop, look, listen, a few days, a few nights, and compare notes."

Fortnum asks what they should be looking for, and Willis replies, "You'll know. You've got to know. Or we're done for, all of us."

By evening, Fortnum has guessed that the Earth is being

invaded and that the mushrooms are somehow involved. When he tells this to his wife, she laughs. How, she asks, could mushrooms without even arms or legs take over the world? Fortnum has no answer. After his wife has gone upstairs to bed, Fortnum goes to the refrigerator for a snack. There, on a shelf in the refrigerator, is a bowl of freshly cut mushrooms. At last comes the crucial realization: The mushrooms infiltrate the human body through the stomach; once he has eaten a mushroom, a human being *becomes* an alien.

Fortnum hears his son working down in the cellar. He calls out to the boy and asks if by any chance he has eaten any of the mushrooms. In a cold, faint voice, Tom replies that he has. Tom then asks his father to come down into the cellar to view the crop. Fortnum knows that by now millions of boys have raised billions of mushrooms around the world. As he stands at the top of the cellar stairs, Fortnum struggles with the incredibility of what he knows to be true: "He looked back at the stair leading up to his wife. I suppose, he thought, I should go say goodbye to Cynthia. But why should I think that! Why, in God's name, should I think that at all? No reason, *is* there?" Fortnum then steps down into the darkened cellar, closing the door behind him.

Since "Zero Hour" and "Mushrooms" are both primarily suspense stories, they share a number of structural traits common to such stories. For instance, the secret of the invasion is revealed to the reader almost at once. Real-life invasions usually depend heavily upon the element of surprise—such as in the attack on Pearl Harbor or in the invasion of Normandy. But in a story it is difficult to sustain reader interest if the main point is concealed until the very end. By revealing the invaders' intentions at the beginning of the story, Bradbury keeps us in constant suspense, wondering if and when the protagonists will catch on. In both stories, the method of invasion is rather improbable. This is necessary because the main character must be teasingly slow in putting the pieces of the puzzle together—but without coming off as an idiot. Because the invaders' plans are quite far-fetched, we can understand it when the main characters rationalize away the threat on the basis of its incredibility and their own need to live in a safe world where such things do not happen.

Both "Zero Hour" and "Mushrooms" focus on a small area. Though the invasions are on a world-wide scale, we see little of what is happening outside the neighborhood of the main characters. An even tighter focus is maintained in the story "Fever Dream" from *A Medicine for Melancholy*. Here again an invasion of Earth by mysterious creatures is taking place. But this time only one person knows, and there is no way he can tell anyone else about it, for the invasion is taking place within his own body.

Thirteen-year-old Charles has been put to bed with what seems to be a bad cold. From the outside, it seems like nothing more. But Charles has begun to experience strange symptoms, which he tries to communicate to his doctor: "My *hand*, it doesn't *belong* to me any more. This morning it *changed* into something else. I want you to change it back, Doctor, Doctor!" Charles's hand shows no external signs of change, and the doctor treats the matter lightly—"You just had a little fever dream." He gives Charles a pill and leaves.

> At four o'clock his other hand changed. It seemed almost to become a fever. It pulsed and shifted, cell by cell. It beat like a warm heart. The fingernails turned blue and then red. It took about an hour for it to change and when it was finished, it looked just like any ordinary hand. But it was not ordinary. It no longer was him any more.

Cut off from his disbelieving parents and the doctor, Charles tries to understand what is happening to him. He recalls how, in a book he once read, ancient trees became petrified as their wood cells were replaced by minerals. On the outside they still looked like trees, but in reality they had changed to stone.

"What would happen," Charles later asks the doctor, if "a lot of microbes got together and wanted to make a bunch, and reproduced and made *more*. . . . And they decided to *take over* a person!" Indeed, Charles has hit upon the truth, but even as he speaks his hands—possessed of a life of their own —crawl up his chest to his throat and begin to strangle him.

Later, alone again, and with his hands strapped to his legs, Charles submits to the progressive take-over of his body. He is trapped more completely than if surrounded by a whole army of soldiers. In a macabre parody of the old wives' cure for insomnia—wherein one relaxes his hands, then feet, then arms, then legs, until theoretically the entire body is relaxed —Charles's body is taken away from him bit by bit. Finally only his head is left, and in silent panic he feels his ears go deaf, his eyes go blind, and "his brain fill with a boiling mercury."

This story is a reversal of the previous stories in which the invaders were, at least in the beginning, external to the victims and brought about an internal psychological struggle. In "Fever Dream," the invasion begins within one person, and after it has conquered him, it moves out into the world at large. Bradbury only touches upon this second phase as Charles, suddenly appearing well again, goes to great lengths to get into physical contact with his parents, the doctor, even his pet parakeet. We realize that Charles is now one of the invaders—a carrier—and is eagerly involved in spreading the invasion. We know too that there will be no clash of armies or weaponry, just the futile struggle of one individual after another with his or her fever dream.

The novel *Something Wicked This Way Comes* is in many ways a novel about invasion. In this case, not about an attack by extraterrestrial aliens, but about the invasion of a small American town by forces of darkness and evil. The story takes place in Green Town, California, setting for many Bradbury short stories as well as the novel *Dandelion Wine*, and roughly patterned after Bradbury's own home town of Waukegan, Illinois.

Green Town is invaded by Cooger and Dark's Pandemonium Shadow Show—on the surface a carnival, but in reality a collection of magicians, witches, and evil-doers long banished from modern society, who come to exercise their powers on Halloween, the one night when they can again hold sway over the Earth. Only two boys and a middle-aged man are aware of the true nature of the carnival, and it falls upon them to repel the invasion. The boys are aptly suited for a battle with magic. Both were born on Halloween—James Nightshade at one minute after midnight, and William Halloway at one minute before. The adult is Charles Halloway, Will's father, the janitor at the public library, a boy who never grew up.

The threat faced by these three is more subtle than an armed military invasion. Because belief in magic, superstition, and fear are individual matters, the danger posed by the carnival is different for every person in town. The carnival draws people to itself by appealing to their unfulfilled needs, their selfishness and cruelty. It holds out to some people the promise of having their deepest wishes fulfilled, then enslaves them with their own greed. Thus the carnival provides itself with a steady supply of new freaks. Charles Halloway eventually realizes that Cooger and Dark's show draws all its energy from the fear and hatred it arouses in its victims, and this gives him the secret he needs to win out.

At the conclusion of *Something Wicked,* Dark, the carnival master, disguises himself as a young boy looking for help, and succeeds in luring Halloway away from Will and Jim. Halloway quickly recognizes that Dark has tricked him to get him alone, but rather than struggle, Halloway suddenly embraces the astonished Dark. Halloway says to himself, "Evil has only the power we give it. I give you nothing. I take back. Starve. Starve. Starve." Without Halloway's fear and hatred to strengthen him, Dark shrivels away to nothing, and the invasion of Green Town comes to a quiet end.

It will be noted that children play important roles in the stories covered so far and in several of those to follow. Bradbury's use of children in general in his stories is too large a subject to treat here. But with respect to stories about invasion, Bradbury seems to agree with the popular concept that children live in a world of their own. Though they occupy the same space as adults do, their perception of it is, in many ways, radically different. They are, in a sense, aliens in their own world. In a story (not about invasion) from the book *Dark Carnival,* Bradbury has a rather paranoid school teacher say to his class, "Sometimes I actually believe that children are invaders from another dimension. . . . You are another race entirely, your motives, your beliefs, your disobediences. You are not human. You are—children." It may not be realistic to view the place of children in the world as in any way sinister, but in Bradbury's hands, it can certainly result in a good story.

Another common element in Bradbury's invasion stories is the theme of metamorphosis. In many stories, such as "Mushrooms" or "Fever Dream," the victim of the invasion undergoes—or prepares to undergo—a change in which he himself becomes one of the invaders. Bradbury frequently plays off of the ambiguity of the relationship between the invader and the invaded. At the moment an invasion succeeds, the invader becomes defender—capable himself of being invaded. In some of the stories about Mars, Earthmen who have begun living on Mars are faced with the fact that they are becoming, naturally enough, Martians. In some cases, the metamorphosis is literal, as in "Fever Dream," but behind this is the metaphorical truth that an invasion may be less of a change of circumstance than a change of mind.

Invasions succeed as often by the demoralization of the invaded as by the simple strength of the invaders. The means by which an invader travels can provide him with an important psychological advantage. In "Mushrooms" and "Fever Dream," Bradbury uses covert, Trojan Horse–type devices in which the invaders arrive in disguise and are not recognized for what they are until it is too late. In other stories, involving Mars and Earth, the invasion device is usually the commonplace but inevitable rocket ship. In *Something Wicked This Way Comes* the forces of evil arrive in a circus train.

Will and Jim witness the train's approach in the dead of night. They suspect that the train is bringing evil to their small town, and these suspicions are confirmed when they hear the train's dreadful whistle:

> The wails of a lifetime were gathered in it from other nights in other slumbering years; the howl of moondreamed

dogs, the seep of river-cold winds through the January porch screens which stopped the blood, a thousand fire sirens weeping, or worse! the outgone shreds of breath, the protests of a billion people dead or dying, not wanting to be dead, their groans, their sighs, burst over the earth!

Sometimes the mere presence of an alien force is enough to destroy a people's will to resist. In "Perhaps We Are Going Away," from *The Machineries of Joy*, an Indian boy, Ho-Awi, awakens to a day that is "evil for no reason." Ho-Awi belongs to a tribe named after a bird that lives near a mountain range named after the shadows of owls. Like the birds that are featured symbolically in their myths, the Indians of the tribe are sensitive to subtle disturbances in natural events.

In the hours before dawn, Ho-Awi joins his grandfather to hunt down the cause of the ominous feeling that pervades the air. They search for evidence that something is amiss in the natural world: "They scanned the prairies, but found only the winds which played there like tribal children all day." At length they approach the shore of the great eastern ocean and Ho-Awi's grandfather catches sight of something that confirms his worst fears. He tells Ho-Awi that a great change is coming, like a change of season. Though it is just the beginning of summer, birds that cannot be seen are flying south. "I feel them pass south in my blood. Summer goes. We may go with it." Ho-Awi asks if this course of things can be stopped or reversed, but the old man, who has already spotted the first encampment of white men on the beach, knows it cannot: "Not you or me or our people can stay this weather. It is a season changed, come to live on the land for all time."

Ho-Awi then sees the white men's camp himself, and realizes his grandfather is right. Not that there is much to see, just the glint of firelight on armor, a few faces, and out on the water "a great dark canoe with things like torn clouds hung on poles over it." But the metal and the ship are evidence of a vast technological gap. So intimidating is this gap that the two Indians who have seen the modest vanguard of the white man's invasion feel their entire world vanishing.

There is no warning they can give that will prepare their tribe for what is to come. Physical resistance may eventually follow, but this will be to no avail, because the psychological battle has already been lost.

Hundreds of years later, in August of 1999, the planet Mars seems enveloped by a similarly disturbing atmosphere. In "The Summer Night," from *The Martian Chronicles,* strange thoughts pop into Martian heads as if from nowhere. In a theater, a Martian woman begins to sing words that are utterly alien to her: "She walks in beauty, like the night / Of cloudless climes and starry skies . . ." All over the planet, similar things occur. Children sing strange rhymes, lovers awaken humming unknown melodies. Women awake from violent nightmares and declare, "Something terrible will happen in the morning." The Martians try to reassure one another before settling into an uneasy sleep. The story ends with a lone night watchman patrolling empty streets and humming a very strange song.

Earthmen, who of course are on the way, do not appear at all in this story. But their presence has already invaded the minds of the telepathic Martians. The outcome of the coming invasion by Earthmen is not stated, but the fact that the Martians are already speaking our language, and find themselves frightened and dismayed by that fact implies that their fate will not be a happy one. The technological level of the Martians is not clear. They seem somewhat like ancient Greeks, attending concerts in marble amphitheaters while children play in torchlit alleys. There is mention of boats "as delicate as bronze flowers" drifting through canals, and of meals cooked on tables "where lava bubbled silvery and hushed." So the Martians obviously have some technological advancement. But the Martians seem to have made a decision about machinery, consigning it to a modest role in their society as an art form, a toy, and an unobtrusive support for a pastoral life style. Though it does not appear in this story, the very existence of a rocket ship en route from Earth to Mars suggests a technology out of sympathy with, and potentially destructive to, the Martian way of life.

We have come to the second major group of Ray Bradbury's invasion stories, those involving the invasion of Mars by Earthmen. Of course, in the tradition of invaders throughout history, when we are doing the invading, it is called "colonization." By having the first Earthmen arrive on Mars in a succession of solitary rockets, Bradbury is able to stage the initial contact of Earthman and Martian several times. Since many of these stories were intended to be read singly, outside the context of a book, the character of the Martians changes to suit the requirements of a particular situation. Thus sometimes the Martians are jealous and brutal, other times they are helpless and complacent. There even seem to be several different intelligent life forms on Mars, each of whom responds to the invaders from Earth in a different way.

The creature in "The One Who Waits," from *The Machineries of Joy*, tells its own story: "I live in a well. I live like smoke in the well. Like vapor in a stone throat . . . I am mist and moonlight and memory . . . I wait in cool silence and there will be a day when I no longer wait." This strange creature has the power, like the giant mushrooms, or the microbes of "Fever Dream" to take possession of other life forms. But this time we experience the story from the creature's point of view.

A rocket lands not far from the well the Martian calls home. Several men approach the well and begin testing the water. The vapor creature allows itself to be inhaled by one of the men:

> Now I know who I am.
> My name is Stephen Leonard Jones and I am twenty-five years old and I have just come in a rocket from a planet called Earth and I am standing with my good friends Regent and Shaw by an old well on the planet Mars.
> I look down at my golden fingers, tan and strong. I look at my long legs and at my silver uniform and at my friends.
> "What's wrong, Jones?" they say.
> "Nothing," I say, looking at them. "Nothing at all."

The tables have been turned; the invader has been invaded. One by one, the creature takes over the bodies and minds of the crewmen from the spaceship. It tries each one out as we might try on a new glove. It enjoys the new sensations the men provide it with of touch, taste, smell. It even has one of the crewmen it is possessing shoot himself so that it can temporarily experience death. Like the boy Charles in "Fever Dream," some of the men try to resist the creature:

> I hear . . . a voice calling deep within me, tiny and afraid. And the voice cries, *Let me go, let me go*, and there is a feeling as if something is trying to get free, a pounding of labyrinthine doors, a rushing down dark corridors and up passages, echoing and screaming.

When it finally tires of its game, the creature kills the remaining crewmen by possessing all of them at once and forcing them to throw themselves into the well. The creature then resumes its post, and quietly waits for the centuries to pass.

One reason the first Earthmen are not very successful invaders is that they make no secret about their coming. There is no secret business in Martian cellars, no exploitation of Martian children. The Earthmen swoop down in noisy rocket ships in broad daylight. To make matters worse, the Martians of *The Martian Chronicles* are telepathic, so they can read the Earthmen's minds before a rocket is even sighted. Thus the Martians have plenty of time to prepare a reception. When the first rocket lands in *Chronicles*, the crew is simply shot to death by a jealous Martian who fears his wife may fall in love with an Earthman. Another expedition lands on what appears to be the outskirts of a small American town. The crew is welcomed by their own mothers, fathers, relatives, and friends—many long thought to be dead. The Martians have, of course, re-created the town and its inhabitants by reading the crewmen's minds. The crew gradually becomes separated as each member is lured off to what he believes to be his old home. Then, one by one, they are killed.

Actual warfare never does break out between men and Martians. By the time Earthmen arrrive in force, most of the Martians have succumbed to diseases from Earth against which they had no immunity. The few Martians remaining abandon their cities and seek refuge in the mountains. The invasion of Mars now goes into full swing. More and more rockets arrive. Lumber and supplies are shipped in, towns are built, and roads are laid connecting them. Benjamin Driscoll, a futuristic Johnny Appleseed, stalks about the planet planting Earth trees. The plains, mountains, and canals of Mars are given new names in honor of rocket pilots, explorers, and remembered places on Earth. The first stage of the invasion is successful: A new population has settled in, and the old population has been driven out. Once the physical invasion has been completed, the more subtle invasion of culture takes place. The Earthmen, like pioneers before them, carry their art, religion, and customs with them. One of the first things an invader does once he has settled on foreign soil is to make his new environment as much like his former home as possible.

In "The Off Season," from *The Martian Chronicles*, the new culture confronts the old. Sam Parkhill opens up a hot dog stand—complete with neon lights and juke box—next to a road he expects will soon be heavily travelled. Parkhill is the personification of the Ugly Earthman: loud, crude, out for the fast buck. One evening a Martian calls on Parkhill. The Martian—a fragile creature, seemingly less substantial than the glass mask and silken robes it wears—has come on a peaceful mission. But the Earthman misunderstands, believing the Martian is attempting to lay claim to the land the hot dog stand occupies. With the arrogance of the conqueror, Parkhill presents the Martian with a few facts of life:

Look here . . . I'm from New York City. Where I come from there's ten million others just like me. You Martians are a couple dozen left, got no cities, you wander around in the hills, no leaders, no laws, and now you come tell me about this land. Well, the old got to give way to the new. That's the law of give and take. I got a gun here . . .

Before Earthmen completely settle on Mars, nuclear war breaks out on Earth. Most of the Earth people on Mars decide to return to the home planet in its time of need. In a very short time, the Earth settlements on Mars are crumbling ghost towns. Bradbury devotes a number of stories to the fate of the few Earthmen left behind on Mars, or the even smaller number who arrive fleeing the war on Earth. Most interesting are those in which the Earthmen undergo the inevitable metamorphosis and become Martians. The last story in *The Martian Chronicles*, "The Million Year Picnic," treats this theme in a matter-of-fact way. The Thomas family—mother, father, and three sons—learn that the Earth has been all but completely destroyed. They symbolically burn a map of the Earth and, gazing at their reflections in a canal, accept their new identities as Martians.

A more poetic treatment of the metamorphosis theme is found in "Dark They Were, and Golden Eyed," from *A Medicine for Melancholy*. Harry and Cora Bittering and their children Dan, Laura, and David arrive with a number of other families to set up a town on Mars. Harry immediately senses something strange about the atmosphere on Mars. "He felt submerged in a chemical that could dissolve his intellect and burn away his past." Harry expresses his misgivings to his wife: "I feel like a salt crystal in a mountain stream, being washed away. We don't belong here."

The Bitterlings and their neighbors build cottages and plant gardens. Each day the rocket from Earth brings the newspaper. Harry reassures himself that all is well: "Why in ten years there'll be a million Earthmen on Mars. Big cities, everything! They said we'd fail. Said the Martians would resent our invasion. But did we find any Martians? Not a living soul! Oh, we found their empty cities, but no one in them. Right?" News of the war on Earth reaches them, and with it the realization that there will be no more rockets for a very long time—that they are in fact trapped on Mars.

Changes slowly begin to occur. The blossoms shaken down from Bitterling's peach tree are not peach blossoms.

The vegetables from the garden begin to taste subtly different. When Harry visits his friend Sam he begins to notice other things.

> "Sam," Bittering said. "Your eyes—"
> "What about them, Harry?"
> "Didn't they used to be grey?"
> "Well now, I don't remember."
> "They were, weren't they?"
> "Why do you ask, Harry?"
> "Because now they're kind of yellow-colored."
> "Is that so, Harry?" Sam said, casually.

Harry is experiencing a phenomenon common to invaders, that of assimilation. Invasion is not merely an intrusion, unless primarily a military operation. When one culture moves in on another, some sort of mixture will probably occur. All cultures need reinforcement to remain alive. When one population invades another and is then cut off from home, the influence of the host culture strengthens. Harry Bitterling is not the first colonial to watch his friends "go native"—but the effect rarely involves a complete transformation into the native species. But this is Mars, and Ray Bradbury's Mars at that. This is a place created by, and subject to, the laws of imagination.

Bitterling's family and friends grow taller, their eyes grow more and more golden. Though they've never been taught it, they begin to use Martian words in their conversations. Harry's son Dan declares he is changing his name to Linnl. Laura and David soon become Ttil and Werr. The transformation takes over all of them like some sweet disease. There is no force, no coercion. As they become Martians, they become more relaxed, more at peace with themselves.

Eventually the former Earthmen abandon their town and move up into the Martian hills. The former Bitterlings occupy a villa in the Pillan Mountains (formerly the Rockefeller Range, formerly the Pillan Mountains). Months later, Bitterling and his wife gaze down at the abandoned Earth settlement in the valley. "Such odd, ridiculous houses the Earth people built," says Harry. His wife answers, "They didn't know any better . . . Such ugly people. I'm glad they've gone."

So the invasion of Mars is over. Bradbury carries his theme of metamorphosis to its ultimate extreme. As in "Fever Dream," and "Boys! Raise Giant Mushrooms . . ." the invader and his victim have become one in the same. Bradbury portrays various life forms—microbe, plant, or human being— moving out from their home worlds to fulfill the need to perpetuate themselves. But he suggests that the price of success might be an ultimate loss of identity. To survive on an alien world, the invader must unite with his victim. Both learn that in order for life to go on, any particular species is expendable, and that the invader's act of aggression may become an act of submission to the higher purpose of life itself.

Bradbury has written only one story in which Martians attempt a military invasion of Earth *à la* H. G. Wells. But the result of the invasion in "The Concrete Mixer" (from the collection *The Illustrated Man*) is quite a bit different from any imagined by Wells. Of course, Wells never saw American pop culture in full flower. Ettil is a peace-loving Martian who only wishes to sit home and read. His fellow Martians are getting ready to invade Earth. Ettil's father-in-law is outraged at Ettil's pacifism: "Who ever heard of a Martian *not* invading? Who!"

Ettil is thrown into prison for draft-dodging. There he is confronted with evidence that he has been reading contraband science fiction magazines from Earth. Ettil readily admits that his sole literary diet has been such fare as *Wonder Stories, Scientific Tales*, and *Fantastic Stories*. He insists that the magazines furnish proof that a Martian invasion of Earth will fail. "The Earthmen know they can't fail. It is in them like blood beating in their veins . . . Their youth of reading just such fiction as this has given them a faith we cannot equal." Ettil is willing to be thrown into a fire along with his beloved magazines rather than join the army, but seeing the disappointment in the eyes of his son, he finally relents.

The Martians are prepared for the worst weapons the Earth might throw at them, but they are quite taken aback by the reception they actually receive. Nurtured on thousands of science fiction stories about invaders from Mars, the Earthmen regard the Martians as superstars. The first rocket to land outside Green Town, is welcomed by the Mayor, by Miss California, a former Miss America, Mr. Biggest Grapefruit in San Fernando Valley, and a brass band playing "California, Here I Come." The rout of the Martian army begins at once. Scarcely have they gotten over being violently ill following helpings of free beer, popcorn, and hot dogs, when they are whisked off to picture shows by amorous women, or pursued by evangelical preachers seeking to save their souls. Ettil is cornered by a Hollywood producer, plied with Manhattans, talked into being technical director for a science fiction film about a wildly improbable Martian invasion. Ettil sinks into a profound depression as he realizes that his fellow Martians are doomed to be lulled by the noisy pleasures of Earth until, one by one, they die in freeway accidents, or of Earth-type afflictions such as cirrhosis of the liver, bad kidneys, high blood pressure, and suicide. Worse, he realizes Earth culture will soon be exported to Mars, and that his quiet home planet will be overwhelmed with night clubs, gambling casinos, and race tracks. One can almost sympathize with poor Ettil when, having stepped into the path of a speeding car being driven by thrill-crazed teenagers, he decides not to get out of the way.

It is not surprising that Ray Bradbury should have written a number of stories about the common science fiction theme of invasion. What is notable is the consistent quality and variety his work exhibits.

Bradbury's stories, like many of his aliens, enter our minds and leave us, perhaps, subtly different from the way we were before.

Timothy O'Reilly

FROM CONCEPT TO FABLE
The Evolution of
Frank Herbert's *Dune*

Imagine a world so dry that one man might kill another for the moisture in his body. From its deep desert, guarded by enormous "sandworms," comes a spice with the power to prolong life and evoke visions of the future. Ten thousand worlds are dependent on that spice—a Galactic Empire, outwardly strong, but rigid and ruled by fear. One man stands against the desert and the Empire. Driven out in the sand to die, he promises the ecological transformation of the water-starved planet and unites its people in a holy war to seize control of the spice, the future, and the Empire.

This is the world of Frank Herbert's *Dune*, considered by many people to be the greatest science fiction novel ever written. Each reader finds a different reason for praise. One is struck by the scope of the creation—an entire world, detailed in topography, ecology, and culture. Another seizes on the relevance of its ecological themes. All are fascinated by the towering characters—epic heroes who sweep their worlds and the reader into their struggles. This is a future one might almost believe has happened, a history stolen from its rightful place millennia hence.

Dune is a novel rich in ideas as well as imagination, though much of the conceptual detail can be missed in the sweep of the action and the emotion of the story. The evolution of some of those concepts in *Dune* can be reconstructed, and the ways that Herbert transformed them into so compelling a story can be pointed out.

Recalling the origins of *Dune*, Herbert says:

> It began with a concept: to do a long novel about the messianic convulsions which periodically inflict themselves on human societies. I had this theory that superheroes were disastrous for humans, that even if you postulated an infallible hero, the things this hero set in motion fell eventually into the hands of fallible mortals. What better way to destroy a civilization, a society or a race than to set people into the wild oscillations which follow their turning over their judgment and decision-making faculties to a superhero?

It was years before the story itself began. Herbert was supporting himself as a newspaper reporter, and his methodical research habits were carried over into his fiction. He created a file-folder on the idea, and accumulated notes on possible scenes and characters to go along with it. For years, he researched the origin and history of religions, trying to understand the psychology by which individuals submit themselves to the juggernaut of a messianic myth. He studied psychoanalysis and philosophy, history, linguistics, economics, and politics, trying to grasp the whole pattern. The initial concept had several incarnations before he finally settled on the story that was to become *Dune*.

Dune sprang, in a way, from Herbert's newspaper work. He had been assigned to write a feature story about an agricultural project in the control of sand dunes. This program, which used an ecological rather than an engineering approach to the problem, was so successful that it was being copied in many other countries, and had attracted considerable attention. Herbert became fascinated by sand dunes, the irresistible way they move, swallowing roads, houses, and on occasion even entire towns. He saw a real drama in the effort to control dunes by planting hardy grasses instead of building walls. The article was never published, but Herbert was hooked, both on ecology and on sand:

I had far too much for an article and far too much for a short story. So I didn't know really what I had—but I had an enormous amount of data and avenues shooting off at all angles to get more. . . . I finally saw that I had something enormously interesting going for me about the ecology of deserts, and it was, for a science fiction writer anyway, an easy step from that to think: What if I had an entire planet that was desert?

Science fiction was the key. It was a medium Herbert had chosen for the "elbow room" it gives. A writer of conventional fiction, unless he is extremely inventive, starts with innumerable givens. His plot must wend its way through them like a road through the contours of a mountain pass. But a science-fiction writer, if he really uses his medium, need take very little for granted. He is not creating a road but an entire world—mountains, pass and all. The problems of sand dune control and desert life which so fascinated Herbert could be fully explored.

He imagined an entire planet that had been taken over by sand, and an ecologist faced with the task of reclaiming it. There too the project begins with dune grass planted on the slip face of the dunes. Gradually other life is introduced in an attempt to start a self-sustaining cycle. World creation had its problems though. Somewhere on the planet, there must be water. It can only be hidden, not completely absent, if the transformation is to be possible. Boldness and imagination gave the author the answer. A native animal acts to trap water—an immature stage of a great predator, the sand-worm. The foreign plants introduced to control the dunes must be poisonous to these "water stealers" if they are to free up moisture for an effective long-term change. And so on, detail by painstaking detail, Herbert constructed a world, in an exercise of ecological imagination as gradual, as delicate, and as complex as such a planetary transformation itself might be.

Herbert also imagined inhabitants for this greatest of deserts. These are the Fremen, who, as befits such a harsh world, are a composite of the most striking qualities of all of Earth's desert dwellers. For their approach to desert survival, Herbert drew heavily on the water-lore of the primitives of the Kalahari, who eke out a living in an utter wasteland by utilizing every drop of water. This was given a science-fiction twist in the imagined technology of the water-conserving "stillsuit" which the Fremen wear, and which reclaims the body's moisture. The culture of the Fremen is drawn most strongly on the Semitic and Arabic models. In an appendix to *Dune* that purports to be a fragment from a future-historical monograph, Herbert says,

> It is vital . . . that you never lose sight of one fact: the Fremen were a desert people whose entire ancestry was accustomed to hostile landscapes. Mysticism isn't difficult when you survive each moment by surmounting open hostility.

Fremen religion bears the stamp of persecution. They are the Jews of the Galactic Empire, always wandering, always awaiting the promised land. This is an important part of their religious makeup, but the formalisms of their religion have more of an Arabic flavor. All of the language, clothing, and customs are Arabic in detail, an overt borrowing that Herbert justifies with a kind of future history showing the interplanetary migrations of these people from long-ago Earth. This allowed Herbert to mix the familiar with the strange, to powerful effect.

As he played with the possibilities, Herbert saw how the two stories he was developing—about the desert world and about the superhero mystique—could come together. In his research, he had noted how the desert is a wellspring of messianic religion. Harsh conditions make for a religion of anticipation, as the history of Judaism demonstrates. Islam, which we tend to associate more than any other religion with a desert environment, has been rocked by continual "Mahdist" movements since its foundation. The political imbroglio involving T. E. Lawrence, to name one recent example, had profound messianic overtones. If Lawrence had been killed at a crucial point in the struggle, Herbert noted, he might well have become a new "avatar" for the Arabs. The Lawrence analogy also suggested to Herbert the possibility for manipulation of the messianic impulses within a culture by outsiders with their own distinct purposes.

At this point, Herbert also realized that ecology might become the focus of just such a messianic episode as he had first envisioned, but here and now, in our culture. "It might become the new banner for a deadly crusade—an excuse for a witch hunt or worse."

Herbert pulled all these strands together in an early version of *Dune*. It was a story about a hero very much like Lawrence of Arabia, an outsider who went native and used religious fervor to fuel his own ambitions—in this case, to transform the ecology of the planet. His plan to reclaim the desert will take hundreds of years. No one then alive will see the fruition of his plan. It is a traditional, future-oriented prophetic pattern.

Somewhere along the line, Herbert saw the limits of this approach. It touched on only one of the dynamics he had uncovered in his research. He had a great many ideas about psychology, the manipulation of power, and the unconscious dynamics of mass movements that he wanted to get into the book. So straightforward a plot was inadequate to carry the burden of everything he wanted to say. He began to layer the story.

Enter Paul Atreides, the hero of *Dune*. He is not merely a prophet, but a here-and-now messiah with more than a visionary dream with which to inspire a following. The story of Pardot Kynes, the ecological prophet of the earlier version, is retained as a subtheme: He plays John the Baptist to Paul's Jesus. Paul takes over the ecological cause when he comes to the planet Arrakis, but he has other axes to grind as well. As does Herbert. In Paul, Herbert has a vehicle to explore the many factors that go into the creation of a messianic "superhero." Herbert lays out in detail the structure of aristocratic leadership, the use of psychological manipulation, the birth of an irresistible legend from individually insignificant events, and an unusual psychogenetic theory of history.

The story begins not in the desert but in the political structure of the Empire. The Empire is ruled, in effect, by an "aristocratic bureaucracy" at the top of a rigid feudal caste system. Paul's father, Duke Leto, hawk-featured, imperious, is a peer of the Galactic Empire and a born leader of men. Leto is forced to Arrakis, the dune world, in a "change of fief" by his hereditary enemy, the Baron Vladimir Harkonnen. Arrakis is a rich planet, but dangerous, and the Baron plans to move against Leto while he is still unsure of his new ground. In this, he has the secret backing of the Emperor, who fears that Leto's superb military cadres excel even his own crack troops. Leto is betrayed and killed soon after his arrival, and Paul is forced to flee to the desert with the Lady Jessica, his mother.

The feudal and paramilitary structure of the Empire and House Atreides reveals an important aspect of what Herbert describes as the superhero mystique. Feudalism is a natural condition into which men fall, he contends, a situation in which some men lead and others, surrendering the responsibility to make their own decisions, follow orders. Duke Leto is generous, bold-hearted, and loved fiercely by all who follow him. Still, he uses them. It is always his purposes, not their own, on which they act. They are maintained—and maintain themselves—as followers, not as equals. This early part of the novel, up to Leto's downfall, depicts Paul's training in the Atreides code. Charisma and loyalty, as well as the fear and propaganda wielded by the Baron, are shown to be tools of statecraft. Herbert later described what he was getting at in this part of the book:

> You gain insights into the moral base upon which Paul makes his own decisions. All of this is couched in a form which makes Paul and his people admirable. I am their advocate. But don't lose sight of the fact that House Atreides acts with the same arrogance toward "common folk" as do their enemies. . . . I am showing you the superhero syndrome and your own participation in it. The arrogant are, in part, created by the meek.

This then is the first layer of the superhero mystique: the hierarchical structure of leadership. Paul is trained to lead and his followers are trained to follow.

At the same time as Herbert was delineating the social structure of the Empire, he was introducing another layer. In the opening scene of the novel, while Paul is still a boy of fifteen, he is tested by a mysterious old woman with the *gom jabbar*—a needle tipped with deadly poison held at his throat while he is subjected to nearly unendurable pain. He must be in total command of his reflexes or die. This is the initiation of the Bene Gesserit Sisterhood, a semisecret organization of women devoted to the devious manipulation of politics and religion. Through the Bene Gesserit, Herbert psychoanalyzes the role of the unconscious in human affairs and the potential for its manipulation by the knowledgeable and unscrupulous. Most people are only half-awake—they react to external stimuli without really knowing why they respond the way they do. By contrast, the Bene Gesserit have schooled themselves to understand and master their own unconscious reflexes. This is graphically demonstrated in the test of the *gom jabbar*, as well as in other almost fantastic feats of psychological and physiological control. In addition, the Bene Gesserit have refined the ability to perceive and to play on the unconscious weaknesses of others. Their power to influence the course of politics depends almost entirely on this ability, applied both to individuals and to groups.

The Bene Gesserits' command over the individual unconscious finds its most acute expression in the power of "voice":

> Hawat started to leap from his chair.
> "I have not dismissed you, Thufir!" Jessica flared.
> The old Mentat almost fell back in his chair, so quickly did his muscles betray him. . . . Hawat tried to swallow in a dry throat. Her command had been regal, peremptory—uttered in a tone and manner he had found completely irresistible. His body had obeyed her before he could think about it. Nothing could have prevented his response—not logic, not passionate

anger . . . nothing. To do what she had done spoke of a sensi-tive, intimate knowledge of the person thus commanded, a depth of control he had not dreamed possible.

"Now you know something of the *real* training they give us," she said.

The significance of this power is easy to miss if we get caught up in the question of whether or not such a thing is possible. Herbert is extrapolating powers of suggestion and psychological manipulation far in advance of anything available today, but the power itself is not the main point. He is saying something about who we are as human animals. In Western civilization, we have placed so much emphasis on conscious thought and rationality that we have forgotten how much of our behavior is unintentional and uncontrolled by consciousness. We make choices for reasons of the flesh and feelings, as well as of the mind. The attraction of the superhero, as Herbert sees it, is a case in point. The Fremen do not follow Paul for logical reasons, but precisely because logic is not enough for comfort in a hostile world. Uncon-scious needs for security, belonging, and surety play a much larger role in a messianic upheaval than the conscious content which masquerades as the "cause."

The Bene Gesserit know that the power to manipulate an individual, however acute, has limited effect on millions. They use legends and superstitions as the mass equivalent to the power of "voice." Their adepts have planted stories on countless planets, insurance against future need. With such a legend as background, it is easy for someone trained as the Bene Gesserit are trained to move an entire world.

When Paul first comes to Arrakis, he walks right into one of these legends. The story tells of the *Lisan al-Gaib*, "the voice from the outer world," who will share the dreams of the Fremen and lead them to fulfillment. Paul is reluctant to play on the legend. It grows around him nonetheless, impelled by the desire of the Fremen for the promised salvation. He does not actively use his powers to call it up, but his superior insight and ability, as observed by the Fremen, set the legend in motion. When Paul first wears a stillsuit, the water-conserving garment of the desert, some intuition tells him how to adjust the fittings correctly, while his father and the other men struggle with the unfamiliar equipment. "He could be the one!" the Fremen whisper. Then Jessica announces that the Atreides will work to bring water to the desert. The legend (which had been twisted by Kynes to include his ecological projections) is once again aroused: "It is said they will share your secret dream." Later, when Paul and Jessica have fled to the desert, they are picked up by a band of Fremen. Though strangers are usually killed for their water, the whispers have already begun to spread, and so the two are taken in. Still, there are doubters, and Paul is challenged to a duel by one of them. Forced against his will to kill the man, Paul weeps for him. This is unheard of on water-starved Arrakis. "He gives moisture to the dead!" the Fremen whisper in awe. Simply by living among them, Paul gives the legend a living presence, and gains power to bend the Fremen to his will. He begins to mold them into a guerrilla force with which to win back his dukedom. But already they are more than that, and so is he. He is no longer Paul Atreides, but Paul Muad'Dib, Mahdi of the Fremen and will-o-wisp of the desert, while his followers have become Fedaykin, "death commandoes." The marriage of a charismatic leader and a people who long to be led has begun to bear its inevitable fruit.

Paul does in fact have remarkable powers, but far more important in the end is how the Fremen respond to them. There is a strong, unconscious projection that makes him even more special than he is. Part of this projection depends on the legends planted by the Bene Gesserit and the way they crystallize around Paul, but even more depends on the faculty of his followers for wishful thinking, the unconscious will to believe there is someone out there with answers they lack. Unable to find adequate strength of purpose in themselves, they look for a truth, a cause, and a leader to supply it. It is the same mutually supportive relationship of leaders and followers which was explored in the feudal setup of House Atreides.

Thus far, Herbert's portrayal of the "superhero syndrome" follows recognizable paths of social and psychological analysis. He drew first of all on the traditional messianic pattern, the longing for a better future exhibited by oppressed peoples. He then showed the structure of leadership—how a society functions with built-in expectations of who will lead and who follow—and explored the nature of charismatic myths and the possibility for manipulation of the unconsciousness in all of us. Each of these was to an extent an extrapolation from accepted understanding. But there is one other concept Herbert built his story on that is unique. This is what we might call his genetic theory of history.

Once again, Herbert uses the Bene Gesserit and the inner powers Paul has gained from them as his vehicle. The source of the almost supernatural abilities of the Bene Gesserit is a substance they call the Truthsayer drug, which allows their Reverend Mothers to draw on profound inner knowledge and the accumulated wisdom of the past. But it is only women who can master the inner changes brought on by the drug. It has always been death for a man. The Bene Gesserit have embarked accordingly on a centuries-long program of selective breeding to produce a man who can take the drug and live. They call their goal the *Kwisatz Haderach*, "the shortening of the way." They hope to open vast new areas to their control—the depths of active male psychology as well as the receptive female. The crippling flaw in the Bene Gesserit skills is that they must be wielded indirectly. They hope that a man fully trained in their esoteric arts would still be able to wield temporal power in a way that they cannot. It is hoped that Paul may be this figure, but he has been born a generation too soon in the plan and is consequently not completely under their control. He has his own destiny to follow.

As it turns out, what Paul's heightened inner powers give him is the same ability to perceive unconscious motivation with regard to masses of people as the Bene Gesserit Reverend Mothers have with individuals. And aided by a process

of "Mentat" computation, he is in effect able to see the
future as the Reverend Mothers see the past. Paul's powers of
prophecy are still latent when the story begins, but they
blossom under the influence of the Fremen diet, which contains massive amounts of melange, the Arrakeen spice to
which the Truthsayer drug is related. In powerful visionary
episodes, Paul breaks through into the swirling matrix of
possibilities that is the future. He sees the forces at work in
the uprising of which he is a part, and understands how
little who he is or what he does has mattered:

> He sampled the time winds, sensing the turmoil, the storm
> nexus that now focussed on this moment place. Even the faint
> gaps were closed now. . . . Here was the race consciousness
> that he had known once as his own terrible purpose. Here was
> reason enough for a Kwisatz Haderach or a Lisan al-Gaib or
> even the halting schemes of the Bene Gesserit. The race of
> humans had felt its own dormancy, sensed itself grown stale
> and knew now only the need to experience turmoil in which
> the genes would mingle and the strong new mixtures sur-
> vive. All humans were alive as an unconscious single orga-
> nism in this moment, experiencing a kind of sexual heat that
> could override any barrier. . . . *This is the climax,* Paul
> thought. *From here, the future will open, the clouds part onto
> a kind of glory. And if I die here, they'll say I sacrificed my-
> self that my spirit might lead them. And if I live, they'll say
> nothing can oppose Muad'Dib.*

Paul calls what he sees in this vision *jihad,* the Arabic word
for the holy war of conquest. He sees his banner at the head
of fanatic legions raging through the known universe. He has
been pursuing limited political aims, but he comes to see that
the forces he has roused cannot easily be laid aside. He had
thought to use them for his own purposes, but he knows before the end that it is he who is being used, as the survival
drives of the race itself seek satisfaction in the upheaval of
war.

In a sense, what Herbert does in Paul's visions is to take
ecological concepts to a much deeper level, as Paul comes to

see the opposition between the aims of civilization and the aims of nature, still represented in the human unconscious. An ecosystem is stable not because it is secure and protected, but because it contains enough diversity that some types of organism will survive despite drastic changes in the environment. It has the strength of adaptability, not of fixity. The effort of civilization, on the other hand, is to create and maintain a kind of security. All too frequently this crystallizes into an effort to minimize diversity and stop change. This is shown at its worst in the rigid structure of the Empire. In essence, what has happened to such a society is that basic survival instincts have been sublimated into the need to *feel* secure. Social structure, religion, messianic dreams—all the factors that go into the creation of a myth—are means by which humans reassure themselves that they are in control of their universe. Yet it is these very factors, taken to an extreme, that contribute to the surrender of conscious control that occurs in the jihad. The mystique of Muad'Dib arises because the people of the Empire are out of touch with the unconscious forces that move them. They do not bend with these forces, but resist them, and on that account are swept away. When it must, the unconscious rages up and has its way. This is the same point as was made in the description of the Bene Gesserit power of Voice: You are controlled by that of which you are unaware and by that which you deny.

In his visions, Paul comes face to face with the universe as it really is, a vastness beyond any hope of human control. Men pretend to power over their fate by creating small islands of light and order, and ignoring the great dark outside. It is this that killed all men who took the Truthsayer drug: They had been conditioned all their lives to an illusion and could not face the reality. Paul confronts the vision of infinity, and learns to yield to it, to ride the currents of infinite time and not to restrain them. And then, symbolically, he leads his troops to victory on the backs of the giant sandworms, the untamable predators of the desert who may yet be ridden by those bold enough to take the risk.

These are difficult concepts—far more serious than are

found in the average science fiction novel—and Herbert went to a great deal of trouble to see that they became more than concepts in the reader's mind. In the novel, the ideas are not presented in a linear manner, as they have been here, but are woven into the texture of plot and imagery and character. When the same idea is shown again and again in many different forms—as with the "superhero" concept—it begins to take on a life independent of any of them.

Herbert is also a master of the use of obscurity and shadow in lending depth to a novel. *Dune* has been so often praised for its fullness of detail that it is easy to overlook the fascination of what has been left out. Certain ideas or scenes that were crucial at one point in the development of the story later dropped out, leaving mysterious signs in the way others are handled. Other significant pieces of background were left deliberately unfinished, to draw the reader's attention deeper into the story and to keep him involved long after it was over. What student of *Dune* has not puzzled over the exact life-cycle of the sandworm, or the history and purposes of the Bene Gesserit? Herbert is endlessly willing to hint, but not to explain. If, as a result, there are ideas that seem to hang unsupported, this only lends fire to the reader's conviction that it is a real world he is exploring, with mysteries that have defied even the author. "The stories that are remembered," says Herbert, "are the ones that strike sparks from your mind one way or another." He tries to strike sparks any way he can.

The book is loaded with symbols, puns, and hidden allusions. Though they may not all be consciously grasped by the reader, they lend weight to the story, a sense of unplumbed depths. For instance, as was noted above, one of the things about sand dunes that initially fascinated Herbert was the irresistible way they move. Though the connection is never explicitly stated, the image of the irresistible juggernaut is central to the book. The dunes brood in the background. Each name, each foreign term, was also chosen with care, sometimes for the sound, sometimes for an association. Others are just for Herbert's own amusement or that of the occasional scholar who will pick them up. Every nuance is meaningful. The Fremen language is adapted from colloquial Arabic, often with significant meanings. Paul's younger sister, for instance, bears the name Alia. She was a member of the Prophet Mohammed's family. The use of colloquial rather than classical Arabic is itself significant, since it is the spoken language that would have survived and evolved over the course of centuries into the Fremen. "Bene Gesserit," though it sounds as if it could be Arabic, is actually Latin. It means "It will have been well done," an apt motto for the scheming Sisterhood. The name Atreides was also consciously chosen. It is the family name of Agamemnon. Says Herbert:

> I wanted a sense of monumental aristocracy, but with tragedy hanging over them—and in our culture, Agamemnon personifies that.

Likewise the name of their enemy, the Baron Vladimir Harkonnen, though in this case the associations are more contemporary. The Russian sound was clearly meant to engage our prejudices—which, it must be remembered; were very much stronger when *Dune* was written in the early Sixties than they are now.

Any one of these details is in itself unimportant, but taken together they cannot help but have an effect. Herbert is trying to engage the unconscious as well as the conscious response of the reader. A further application of this principle is his use of rhythm. Herbert is convinced that the sound of a passage is subconsciously reconstructed by the reader even though he reads silently, and furthermore, that it has a powerful unconscious effect. As a result, he wrote a great many crucial passages in the book as poetry—sonnets, haiku, and many other different forms depending on the mood—and then concealed them in the prose. On a larger scale, he very carefully controlled the pacing of the book to underscore the sexual nature of the jihad. The ending of *Dune* is a tour-de-force, in which action, character, and themes are brought to an explosive climax. Literally. Herbert admits:

It's a coital rhythm. Very slow pace, increasing all the way through. And when you get to the ending, I chopped it at a non-breaking point, so that the person reading skids out of the story, trailing bits of it with him.

The end result of all this art is a novel packed with ideas that cannot easily be shaken from the mind. This is more than good entertainment. Herbert has said that the function of science fiction is not always to predict the future but sometimes to prevent it. Many of the features of the superhero mystique that he unveils in *Dune* haunt our own culture. By increasing our awareness of a problem, science fiction can be a powerful tool for change. When it reaches the subconscious levels where the old, inappropriate response patterns are rooted, as *Dune* so clearly does, it goes beyond being even a cautionary fable and becomes, in Herbert's own words, a "training manual for consciousness."

Barbara J. Bucknall

ANDROGYNES IN OUTER SPACE

When Ursula Le Guin published *The Left Hand of Darkness* in 1969, androgyny was not a popular theme. And yet her tale of a frozen planet full of androgynous aliens who go into *kemmer* (as they call oestrus) once a month, becoming male or female through a chemical interaction with their partners, but remaining neuter the rest of the time, struck the imagination of the reading public immediately and earned her the Hugo and Nebula Awards. The idea seemed to be a wonderful solution to so many of the problems that exist between women and men.

If there were no real distinction between women and men, there could be no put-downs, no fear, no arrogance, no mistrust between the sexes, no double standard. There would be no shame attached to pregnancy or burden attached to motherhood, since everyone at some time would be running the same chance. There would be no shame or hesitation about seeking sexual fulfillment, since the imperative nature of the biological need would be recognized by all alike. There would be no sex roles, no stereotypes, so love could always be expressed physically in terms of the real nature of one's emotions. And everybody could have their turn at every form of procreation, begetting and giving birth. Old enmities and misunderstandings would be forgotten, and there would be unity and union. Peace on earth! Goodwill to women as well as to men!

In her essay "Is Gender Necessary?" published in *Aurora:*

Beyond Equality (ed. Vonda N. McIntyre and Susan Janice Anderson, 1976), Le Guin insists that androgyny is not the main theme of the book, the main theme being rather that of fidelity and betrayal. But, quite apart from the instantaneous response that the idea of the androgyne evokes in the reader's imagination, there has to be a reason, and a reason that makes good sense in creative terms, for using the androgyne as a term of reference for the discussion of fidelity and betrayal. The androgyne, simply by being presented as existing, looks to the trusting and warm-hearted reader like the answer to a question, and that answer looms so large that the theme of fidelity and betrayal tends to get pushed a little to one side. If one thinks about the androgyne for a long time and investigates the full implications of *The Left Hand of Darkness*, the theme of fidelity and betrayal does, in fact, have importance. I mean to come back to that later. But it is not what strikes the reader at first glance.

The androgyne looks to a lot of us like an answer. But, as the saying goes, "What is the question?" This whole issue of questions and answers is so important to Ursula Le Guin that she makes it a central feature of the Handdara, a mystical cult she has invented so that her androgynes can have a religion. (In fact, they have two, for there is also the Yomesh cult.) The Foretellers of the Handdara have perfected the art of accurate prediction in reply to any answerable question. Their visitor from earth, Genly Ai, is fascinated by this skill and asks why more use is not made of it—for instance, for advising governments. The Foreteller whom he is questioning replies that they make these predictions purely and simply to show how useless it is to know the answers to the wrong questions. And this seems to be very much a tenet of Le Guin's own philosophy. When faced with her androgyne, we have to ask the right questions.

In "Is Gender Necessary?" Ursula Le Guin suggests some directions that we could reasonably take in approaching this issue. It seems that when she first started to work with the notion of the androgyne, it was because she felt a need to define more exactly what gender and sexuality meant for her personally. Something was going on in the subconscious, for Ursula Le Guin and for many other women, that needed to be made conscious. Writing *The Left Hand of Darkness* was, she says, a kind of thought-experiment. By sending a conventional young man from Earth into a culture where there was no sexual differentiation, she made it possible for herself to imagine an area of humanity that would be shared by both sexes alike. She sums up the results of her experiment by saying that there is no war on her imaginary planet, although war is beginning to be a possibility, no exploitation, and no means of using sexuality as a determining social factor. Finally, she concludes by saying that, although an androgynous society would have problems (since all societies always do), our destructive dualisms, based on a structure of ownership and dominance, which she sees as based on gender, would give way to a healthier, more integrated mode of life. In other words, the male and female elements, instead of being in conflict, would be in harmony. We are alienated, in her opinion, because we have separated the Yang (the masculine element) from the Yin (the feminine element), and our greatest need is to bring the two together.

This suggests that perhaps the questions we should start to ask about the androgyne should be framed in psychological, philosophical, and even religious terms, rather than in terms of biology and desire. In fact, any reader of *The Left Hand of Darkness* who wants to know very much in any detail about the biological functions of the androgyne is liable to be disappointed, since the basic information Ursula Le Guin provides on the subject is summed up in a couple of pages, in a style as blunt and dry as that of a medical text. We hear far more about the myths and legends and religious beliefs of the androgynes than we do about their biology. Ursula Le Guin says "he" and "his" and refers to her androgynes as men, because "he" is the generic pronoun. In those myths and legends, romantic love is very important. But there is far more explicit sexuality in the average women's magazine than in this book.

Although Le Guin insists that sex on her imaginary planet,

Gethen, is remarkably guilt-free, this does not mean that the result is total license. She suggests various interesting reasons for this, but perhaps the most important is that her androgyne is a symbol of integration and wholeness. When she speaks of the alienation of the Yang from the Yin in our society, she is very serious, and she makes it quite clear in the course of her novel that the androgyne represents the Yang and the Yin once more in accord.

When Genly Ai, the visitor from Earth who is acting as the envoy of the Ekumen, or League of Worlds, arrives in Karhide with an invitation for Gethen to join the Ekumen, he receives assistance in his mission from Therem Harth rem ir Estraven, Prime Minister of Karhide. However, Estraven falls from power, and Genly, who is implicated in his disgrace, feels betrayed by Estraven, whom he does not understand or trust. The envoy tries again to interest people in his mission, this time in the neighboring state of Orgoreyn, where Estraven has already sought refuge. There, he is disowned by the faction that at first supported him. Greatly to his surprise, for, in spite of Estraven's warnings, he expected no betrayal, he finds himself in a forced labor camp, from which he is rescued, again to his surprise, by Estraven. The two of them set out to cross a frozen wilderness to return to Karhide, and on the way real trust and love grow up between them. However, there is a feeling on both sides that it would be inappropriate to express this in sexual terms. It is toward the end of this journey that the Yang-Yin symbolism is explained. Genly draws the ancient Chinese symbol of the double curve inside a circle, one half white and the other black. The white side stands for the Yang principle, which is light, masculine, and active. The black side stands for the Yin principle, which is dark, feminine, and receptive. The two sides together represent the reconciliation of opposites, conforming to each other's outline in perfect harmony. Repeating a line from an old Gethenian poem that Estraven had quoted to him earlier in their journey, Genly says, "*Light is the left hand of darkness* . . . how did it go? Light, dark. Fear, courage. Cold, warmth. Female, male. It is yourself, Therem. Both and one. A shadow on snow."

Patterns based on old Chinese ways of thinking are very important in this book. Le Guin acknowledges as much in "Is Gender Necessary?" Yin-Yang symbolism is absolutely basic to the traditional Chinese view of life, and is found alike in Taoism, which Le Guin has named, on more than one occasion, as her preferred philosophy, and in the *I Ching* or *Book of Changes,* to which she also refers from time to time and which was closely studied by Confucius.

In this interest, Le Guin is not alone. Ever since the fifties, there has been an interest in North America in Taoism, in Zen Buddhism (which is related in outlook and approach to Taoism), and in the *I Ching.* This interest has been considered by those who do not share it as manifesting a disquieting anti-intellectualism and antirationalism that is part of a collective approach to insanity. But, in fact, it really represents an attempt to achieve a holistic outlook in which the reason and emotions are no longer divided, and the solution to problems is sought with the full wholeness of one's being. It is for seekers of this kind that Le Guin writes, because she shares their search.

The *I Ching,* which is considered by many to be a fortune-telling book, consists of sixty-four hexagrams composed of solid (Yang) and broken (Yin) lines. The first hexagram in the book, Ch'ien, the Creative, consists of six solid lines. The second, K'un, the Receptive, consists of six broken lines. Male and female, in their pure state, thus appear at the beginning of the *I Ching,* and all the subsequent hexagrams represent the various combinations resulting from their encounter. Thus everything is male-female in varying degrees. Each line in each hexagram has a special meaning, and one consults the *I Ching* to find the hexagram appropriate to one's situation by casting yarrow stalks or, more rapidly, coins.

Genly refers to this practice when he goes to consult the Foretellers of the Handdara and tries to understand how they arrive at their predictions and what chance they have of being right. As he wonders what question to put to the Foretellers, in order to test them, he takes into account the information that the Foretellers could give a yes-or-no answer to a question on a subject of which they were, in their normal state, quite ignorant. "This seemed to put the business on the plane of pure chance divination, along with yarrow stalks and flipped coins," he says, but he is assured that it is in fact not a matter of chance.

This reference to the *I Ching* is doubly ironic, for while Genly is being ironic about yarrow stalks and flipped coins, Le Guin is being ironic about him and his attitudes, as she frequently is throughout the book. The would-be rationality he brings to the subject of foretelling is typical of the defensiveness he exhibits throughout the book, until he finally learns to love and trust Estraven and, through him, Gethenians in general. But the *I Ching* is not the main point at issue here, for the Handdara cult bears a very strong similarity to Taoism. As the Taoist places the highest value on the Void, the adept of the Handdara gives praise to "Darkness and Creation unfinished" and studies how to achieve ignorance. Such a statement is easily misunderstood by the would-be rational Western mind, so Le Guin explains (although not immediately) what is meant by ignorance in this sense. It is "to ignore the abstract, to hold fast to the thing." The whole training of the Handdara teaches the adept to avoid looking for answers or even paying attention to them once they have been given. "Nusuth"—"no matter"—is a typical Handdara response to most issues. Estraven, who has received Handdara training, is remarkable for his ability to react, immediately and with his whole being, in a way that is totally appropriate to any given situation. In this, he leaves Genly, who has to puzzle out the answer to problems, far behind.

We could take this as a reference to feminine intuition, but as an approach it is markedly Taoist. However, it is fair to say that Taoism leans traditionally to the feminine side and has been, in consequence, in opposition from the start to the philosophy of Confucius, which is more masculine and authoritarian. The political systems of Gethen, by the way, reflect the creative tension between the Taoist and the Confucian, since they are based on an authoritarian form of government—monarchy or bureaucracy—which is modified by individual anarchism. The Gethenian is an instinctive anarchist—and so, according to Le Guin, feminine—everywhere except in Orgoreyn, where troublemakers are drugged and bullied into submission. The Yomesh cult, which constitutes an aberration from the point of view of the Handdarata, since it insists that all answers were revealed in one moment of time to its founder, the Foreteller Meshe, counts followers in Karhide but appears to be the established religion in Orgoreyn. This is in itself significant. Karhide, as the less power-and-answer-oriented of the two states appears preferable to Orgoreyn. However, we do have to recognize that it is from Karhide that the threat of Gethen's first real war is beginning to come, at the moment when Estraven, who wishes peace, is overthrown and proscribed.

Le Guin gets rather tired of people who talk too much about her moral values and harp on her feeling for wholeness and balance—there is something peculiarly infuriating about having a glib, easy lip service paid to values that have been worked out through personal struggle and pain. And apart from that, Le Guin, like any strong personality, has her dark side and recognizes it in other people, including the people she invents. Symbol of wholeness as her androgyne may be, the Gethenian is a human being, and consequently as subject to weakness, error, folly, and even crime as any other person. There is no war, but feuds and murder are fairly common, and every feature of Gethenian life is controlled by a stylized form of one-upmanship called *shifgrethor*, which is related to the old Chinese concept of face and face-saving, and which Genly, accustomed as he is to the masculine ego, finds baffling and annoying.

Estraven, who is presented in the most sympathetic light as a truly admirable human being, capable of continence in the midst of *kemmer*, trained to perform enormous feats of strength and endurance through sheer willpower, showing exceptional ingenuity and perseverance in the midst of every possible rebuff and failure, true to his purpose, to his love, and to his friend—this Estraven has, by the day of his death, committed every crime the Gethenians most deeply despise.

He is considered a traitor to Karhide because of his willingness to cede territory in a border dispute. In addition to this, he is so determined to help Genly in his mission that, in order to make Gethen join the Ekumen, he is willing to sacrifice the prestige (or *shifgrethor*) of Karhide. And since politics on Gethen is played on the level of *shifgrethor*, this is a very real betrayal from the point of view of the king of Karhide. Betrayal, in a way, runs in Estraven's family, because one of his ancestors, whose tale is told in one of the "documents" with which the narrative is interspersed, was known as Estraven the Traitor for ceding territory in order to end a feud. The Estraven of the present story bears his ancestor's first name, Therem.

The betrayal in question obviously consists of the subordination of family or national interests to the larger interests of mankind. Even more deeply despised than betrayal is theft —and Estraven steals food, at the outset of their journey across the ice, to keep himself and Genly alive. And the worst of all crimes is suicide, which Estraven commits by skiing straight into the guns of the border guards who have been posted to kill him. But perhaps his worst offense, from our non-Gethenian point of view, is his incestuous love for his brother, to whom he vowed *kemmering* (or life-long fidelity) in their youth and with whom he has had a child. In itself, an incestuous relationship with a brother is permissible on Gethen, but the lovers are not allowed to vow *kemmering* or to remain together after the birth of a child. It seems that Estraven and his brother left their clan-home (or Hearth) in order to preserve their relationship, after the birth of their child. The brother is dead and the indications are that he committed suicide.

Incest, in fact, is a central theme in *The Left Hand of Darkness*, and it is largely in terms of incest that the idea of the androgyne is linked to the theme of fidelity and betrayal. Structurally, this is extremely important, because the basic situation on Gethen is somehow incestuous. At the beginning of the book, Estraven tosses off the epigram that "Karhide is not a nation but a family quarrel," and this turns out to be true. The basic social unit in Karhide is the Hearth, which is the home of the clan, and every social institution on Gethen is based in some form on the Hearth—even the Commensality of Orgoreyn, which is a lifeless, loveless, schematized imitation of the close-knit, quarrelsome, loving, flesh-and-blood relationship exemplified by the Hearth. But, even apart from that, Gethenians are so close to each other in their basic outlook that sex between Gethenians must always be closer to sex between brother and sister (since Gethenians always mate as man and woman) than any other sexual bond. Into this situation comes the Alien, the Stranger, and breaks the incestuous bond. Fidelity to the Stranger means betrayal of the family.

The old Gethenian myths and legends scattered throughout the narrative counterpoint the relationship between Genly and Estraven in terms of a symbolism that is connected with the details of their journey across the ice. This is particularly marked in "The Place Inside the Blizzard," the tale of incest that occurs, quite abruptly and unexpectedly, in the second chapter. At first it appears to have no connection with the preceding chapter, in which Genly records his belief that Estraven has let him down. But the juxtaposition of the themes of betrayal and incest, at the outset of the book, ensures that they will be connected in the reader's mind, although, in all probability, at the unconscious level. Two brothers vow *kemmering*, against the taboo. When a child is conceived, they are ordered to part, and the brother who bears the child commits suicide. The other brother, who is considered responsible for the suicide, is driven from the Hearth, but returns to curse it and announces that he too will commit suicide. He goes out on the ice and travels through a snowstorm until he reaches the place inside the blizzard where he no longer feels cold or pain and everything, including himself, seems to be made of snow. Here his dead brother comes to meet him and says that this is the place where they will keep their vow. But the dead brother cannot speak the living brother's name, and this frightens the living brother, who says he will not stay and who reproaches the suicide for killing himself instead of leaving the Hearth with him and keeping their vow in concealment. The living brother runs away and survives, although his left hand, which had been seized by the dead brother, is frost-bitten and has to be amputated. As an old man, shortly before his death, he takes back the curse from his Hearth, and reconciliation is finally brought about.

The next tale of prohibited love is in chapter nine, which tells how Estraven the Traitor was born to the heirs of two feuding families and finally ended the feud, ceding land and killing some of his own clan. This story is told in terms of love at first sight and of people fated to come together. The left and right hands of the ill-fated lovers and of the surviving parent and child match exactly, which proves in emotional terms their predestined affinity. The last of these tales of love and death comes in chapter seventeen, where we get an Orgota creation myth. (Tales from Karhide are balanced against the teachings of Orgoreyn). This myth tells how the first man kills all his brothers but one and couples with his surviving brother in a house built of the frozen bodies of the others. Because his children are born in the house of flesh, each is followed around by a piece of darkness—his shadow. In the end, only darkness will remain. This myth counterpoints chapter twelve, "On Time and Darkness," which expresses the Yomesh belief that "in the Sight of Meshe there is no darkness" and that there is no source or end.

So the Gethenian myths and legends illustrate the theme of incest and also the themes of love and betrayal, left and right, light and darkness, shadow and snow, birth and death, revelation and ignorance, beginning and end, and the denial of end and beginning. They are all summed up by a scrap of an old poem, *Tormer's Lay*, which does not form the subject of a separate chapter but which is quoted by Estraven to Genly in chapter sixteen:

> *"Light is the left hand of darkness*
> *and darkness the right hand of light.*
> *Two are one, life and death, lying*
> *together like lovers in kemmer,*

like hands joined together,
like the end and the way."

But the first tale, the incest legend, remains dominant. Even as Estraven quotes *Tormer's Lay*, his voice shakes, for he remembers that in the letter his brother wrote him before his death he had quoted the same lines. When the two fugitives set out on their journey across the ice, Estraven tells Genly that the good weather tends to stay over the great glaciers, while the storms are pushed out to the periphery, and that this accounts for the legends about the Place inside the Blizzard. This is a direct reference to chapter two and indicates that Estraven is going in search of his dead brother. In fact, he does find him, in chapter eighteen, when Genly teaches Estraven telepathic communication, or, as he calls it, "mindspeech," and speaks Estraven's name, in mindspeech, with the dead brother's voice. This is particularly striking as, in the legend, the dead brother could not speak the living brother's name, and it implies that the curse of hopeless and prohibited love has somehow come to an end. Also left and right are affirmed together, instead of the left hand of the living brother being destroyed. Finally, in the last chapter, when Genly comes to Estraven's Hearth to speak of his dead friend to Estraven's parent and child, this represents a hope for new beginnings.

In *The Left Hand of Darkness*, Ursula Le Guin has told, in terms of far greater complexity and ambiguity, substantially the same tale as she had told in *The Tombs of Atuan*. In the earlier work, which is told in mythical terms so that the outlines have to be very clear, a young girl has been brought up to serve the forces of darkness. She has in her power a wizard, a wise and good man who serves the forces of light. She could destroy him but, almost in spite of herself, she chooses to save him and escape with him from the realm of night. In so doing, she saves herself. Symbolically, this depicts the young girl's decision to trust herself to a man for the first time, and this decision is shown in very optimistic terms. In *The Left Hand of Darkness*, things are not so clear.

The sexual nature of the relationship between Genly and Estraven is blurred by the fact that Estraven is an androgyne who is neuter most of the time and Genly seldom has the opportunity to see him as a sexual being. But when he does, it is significant that he sees Estraven as a woman. As in *The Tombs of Atuan*, it is the "female" partner who contrives the male partner's escape. But Genly is very far from being the wise mage who serves the forces of light, and Estraven is by no means in the grip of the powers of darkness, but represents, in his own being, the reconciliation of darkness and light. Finally, there is no living happily ever after, for, in order to complete Genly's rescue, Estraven has to die, and in order to bring his mission to a successful conclusion, Genly has to break his promise to Estraven to clear his name. Love, although the one thing needful, is no longer a triumphant solution, but in itself, a source of grief and pain. And there is fidelity and betrayal on both sides.

The maturity of this conclusion to *The Left Hand of Darkness* chastens the reader somewhat, reducing the euphoria felt on first meeting the idea of the androgyne. The longing for a lost completeness, for, as Plato puts it, "the desire and pursuit of the whole," the nostalgia for a once-upon-a-time when all went well may, it seems, be a trap, a return to the incestuous bonds of childhood. But, since everything is double-natured (the Yin and the Yang again), this trap may be sprung and a way found out of it into greater harmony. As Estraven points out, duality is part of the androgyne, for there is always the Other. Recognition of the Other is the lesson of innocence and experience alike, and through this recognition we reach maturity.

In other words, Le Guin leaves us with an insight that is as classical as her way of presenting it is unorthodox. This is, basically, what makes *The Left Hand of Darkness* a work different in nature from other well-known thought-experiments in human sexuality. When Aldous Huxley described new types of sexual relationships in *Brave New World*, he was expressing, quite directly, his abhorrence of promiscuity and his angry regret that old sexual patterns were changing. And when Joanna Russ wrote *The Female Man,* she was being just as direct about her resentment of men and her approval of a world that would be full of strong, healthy, happy, loving lesbians. Again, when Samuel R. Delany describes, in *Triton,* the dilemma of Bron Helstrom, who is hopelessly confused about his sexual role because he is looking for a woman who will conform to a female stereotype that has long since disappeared, Delany is quite direct in showing his disapproval. Helstrom actually has a sex change in order to turn himself into the kind of woman he thinks he wants and then finds that the kind of man who wants that kind of woman no longer exists (since he cannot be two people at once).

In fact, the comparison of *Triton* with *The Left Hand of Darkness* is quite illuminating, because the possibility of homosexuality is open to Helstrom, if he feels incapable of a heterosexual relationship, both as a man and as a woman, and his possible homosexual partners are presented as kindly people who are genuinely fond of him, whereas homosexuality is to all intents and purposes ruled out in *The Left Hand of Darkness.* There is such a thing as perversion on Gethen, however. Certain Gethenians remain in *kemmer* all the time and are called Perverts—quite logically, since constant *kemmer* supposes a sexual obsession that must be repulsive to those who are free from it. Without realizing it, Genly adopts this attitude, and when his companions finally arrive from their starship, he sees them as repulsively sexual.

Le Guin gets annoyed when critics reduce the substance of her books to some simple message, which she likens to a fortune cookie motto, but there is no denying that the simple message is there. One of the things we get from *The Left Hand of Darkness* is a parable about wanting one-sentence answers to the meaning of life. When Genly visits the Foretellers, he is told about the origin of the Yomesh cult. A certain lord once forced a group of Foretellers to answer the question, "What is the meaning of life?" The Foretellers took six days and nights to answer it. At the end, some were catatonic, some were dead, one had murdered the questioner, and the leader of the group, Meshe, had received the total insight that enabled him to found his cult. The adepts of the Handdara apparently find this story very funny, which, according to Taoist principles, they should. The Taoist who has received enlightenment does not go around making earth-shaking prophecies or founding cults, but is liable to say something quite ordinary, such as "Will you have a cup of tea?" But he does this in a way that is so totally appropriate to the situation that the person to whom he is offering the cup of tea is profoundly impressed and may even receive enlightenment too. In such circumstances, it seems, even a fortune cookie motto can be enlightening.

5

Catherine Podojil

SISTERS, DAUGHTERS, AND ALIENS

It is a literary irony that although the first work of science fiction is generally agreed to be Mary Shelley's *Frankenstein*, published in 1818, women writers have until very recently avoided the genre as they have no other branch of serious fiction. There are exceptions, of course. Many respectable contemporary science fiction anthologies include at least one story by any of several women writers: Judith Merril, Leigh Brackett, Andre Norton, Zenna Henderson, Ursula Le Guin, and several others. But there is usually only one (and often the same one) out of twelve to fifteen selections.

In addition, readership studies conducted by the leading science fiction publications show that women don't read it either. Up to 90 percent of the readers of magazines in the field are males, specifically adolescent males.

There are several probable explanations for this dearth of writing and readership. The most obvious is the subject matter of science fiction. The combination of technological pursuits and fast-moving, violent action performed by male characters, which constitutes much of twentieth-century science fiction, is one that appeals traditionally to boys and men, and not to girls and women. Women have written, and read, genres that are strong on character, internal reality, and the circumstances that constitute everday living.

In consequence, women writers in the field of science fiction have often found themselves adopting traditionally male techniques or points of view. Some writers changed or disguised their names, making them at least neuter, if not male. Some wrote according to prescription—violent action with male protagonists.

It is even more of an irony that Mary Shelley set the stage for what was to come. Though the particular character of contemporary violence is not found in her work, she did write a novel about technological concerns in which the only characters of any interest are men, and she wrote from a male point of view. This is not to condemn her or her work, which has no superior and few equals in the genre, but to point out a social and literary pattern.

Despite these difficulties, the science fiction genre appears to offer a perfect format in which to explore new ways of acting and thinking free of current thought regarding power, childbearing, technology, and other concerns of women.

Or does it? It is suggested in a fine series of essays by Pamela Sargeant in her *Women of Wonder* books (Vintage Books) that science fiction is not nearly as original or liberating a genre as is commonly believed. Sargeant maintains that, in fact, its values and social structures are more closely tied to those of the prevailing culture than has been previously supposed.

Despite the pitfalls, however, women have written science fiction, some in any period, and many more of late. The questions for discussion in this essay are: What are the specific themes that women explore when they write science fiction from a feminist point of view? Are there recurring patterns that can be contrasted with those of the traditional masculinity of the genre, or even patterns that stand alone without a symmetrical balance on the masculine side? And, if the works considered are written during different historical eras, are there differences in attitudes that may be attributed to this fact?

We have undergone the beginnings of a new feminist renaissance in the past decade that has called into question virtually all existing values and has seen the entrance of women into social, political, and artistic disciplines in which they were previously unwelcome. The field of science fiction is no exception. The writers considered in this essay are Joanna Russ, James Tiptree, Jr., and Sondra Dorman, all of whom have written the bulk of their work within the framework of the recent feminist movement, and Judith Merril, whose short novel *Daughters of Earth* was published in 1953. The works by the former group, short stories all, include Russ's "When It Changed," Tiptree's "The Women Men Don't See" and "Houston, Houston, Do You Read?" and Dorman's "Building Block." A note about James Tiptree, Jr.—she has recently identified herself as Alice Sheldon, who also writes under the name Racoona Sheldon.

Judith Merril's *Daughters of Earth* is the first chronologically, and is important for the period in which it was written, a period in which support for feminist ideals was very limited. What Merril does here is—casually and without fanfare— to assert the primacy of daughters in history, specifically the history of exploration and resettling of new worlds. This, more than any other element, is what sets her work apart from other science fiction and much of Western fiction in general. History can be seen as the doing of deeds by men, who then set those deeds down on paper to pass on to and inspire the future, i.e., sons, grandsons, and generations of other male doers. In *Daughters of Earth,* the focus is on women who leave the nest, travel outward to new lands, contribute an equal share of knowledge and hard physical work to the new civilizations, and bear daughters who will continue the creation.

The format of the novel is conventional science fiction— the movement of earth people to the planets and outward, using spaceships and space stations, encountering alien lands and beings, dealing with isolation, homesickness and other problems. The departure from convention is that the point of view is female, as are most of the important characters. The narrator, Emma Tarbell, is the daughter of the third generation, who uses a variety of points of view, including her own in a journal, to tell her story to her granddaughter, the daughter of the fifth generation. Emma was born on Uller, a planet beyond Pluto in our solar system. Her own mother came to Pluto from earth. Now Emma's granddaughter Carla will emigrate farther out into the unknown in company with other humans, as well as the aliens on Uller with whom the humans have established a form of communication.

It would be inaccurate to say that *Daughters of Earth* contains no important male characters, for it does. But their experiences, as well as those of the women, are seen through the eyes of women and then passed on by them. It is the female point of view that selects from and arranges all the aspects of reality. Taking off from the Bible's Book of Genesis, surely as masculine a work reflecting as masculine a world as exists in the Western tradition, *Daughters of Earth* opens with the words "Martha begat Joan, and Joan begat Ariadne. Ariadne lived and died at home on Pluto, but her daughter Emma took the long trip out to a distant planet of an alien sun. Emma begat Leah, and Leah begat Carla, who was the first to make her bridal voyage through sub-space, a long journey faster than the speed of life itself."

In a symmetry that rings true both artistically and realistically, every other daughter is a homebody, both needing and providing security, so that her daughter can be free or rebellious enough to risk the new and the untried. Merril was aware of the difficulties then, as now, of integrating the desires for security and risk that reside in the female psyche. Emma, the narrator and a traveler herself, says to Carla, the recipient of the journal, "There are such similarities, Carla dear, between Joan Thurman and myself, between me and you. And on the other side, there is such a pattern of identity between Martha and (Ariadne) and (Leah). It seems to me there should be some way of braking the pendulum swing . . . of producing, sometime, a child who is neither rebelliously 'idealistic' nor possessively demanding of security in its most obvious form."

But Merril can't refrain from making clear her own preference for the life of adventure, as Emma continues, "Perhaps the others—Leah and Ariadne and Martha—perhaps they knew some happiness I never understood; but I am certain that they never knew the kind of total purpose in living that has been my great joy."

Merril's daughters make their mark within the framework of traditional heterosexual love and marriage. The traveling daughters have husbands who are partners with them in adventure; the nesting daughters have good and decent husbands wherever they nest—earth, Pluto, or Uller. In this belief that the exploration of space will in its arduousness demand equality between men and women, Merril is showing more optimism than most contemporary feminists would. But within the framework of a genre that almost always sees women, if at all, as breeders and sex objects, *Daughters of Earth* is a breakthrough.

The book considers a theme that some of the other selections take up in more detail. Again, in an almost offhand way, Merril creates a social order in which the values traditionally associated with men, or at least maleness, are not suffocatingly present. War and aggression are absent, though conflict, confrontation, and struggle are not. Men do not need to be in charge, though some are, as are many women. Leadership seems to be based on what the colony needs at any given time; power struggles are between intellectual or theoretical disciplines. There is no rape. The conflict between generations is not Oedipal and violent, but is acted out between mother and daughter, though not without pain and unhappiness.

This is not to say that other traditional values are not present. Occasional reference is made to undesirable traits in a woman who wants to marry. Emma recalls ". . . it had been firmly concluded at home some time before that I was doomed to single bliss. Too direct, too determined, too intellectual, too *strong;* no man would feel up to it . . ." according to her mother. And later on, we see the point of view of Emma's daughter, Leah: "She did not understand how her mother could be so stupid as to try to attract a man by being *bright.*" In reality she is not trying to attract anyone; she is simply doing her job, which she loves and does well. But her daughter is more concerned about traditional values.

Two other elements of *Daughters of Earth* deserve some attention. Science fiction is historically a white, as well as a male, genre. To call it racist is not overexaggerating. Not only are the protagonists white and mostly Aryan or offshoots thereof, but the alien invaders encountered everywhere are described in terms that make us cringe in embarrassment today. Ursula Le Guin says in an essay, "Military virtues are taken as ethical ones. Wealth is assumed to be a righteous goal and a personal virtue . . . In general American SF has assumed a permanent hierarchy of superiors and inferiors, with rich, ambitious aggressive males at the top. Then a great gap, and then at the bottom the poor, the uneducated, the faceless masses and all the women . . ."

At the bottom, of course, are all those people with names such as Levine, Toglio, Gorevitch, and Cabrini. But in Merril's book all these are people who accompany Emma Tarbell to Uller to set up a new colony. So Merril must be given credit for recognizing the value of ethnicity long before it was fashionable and for her casual way of suggesting that any legitimate space exploration that does not include people other than the Smiths and the Joneses is ridiculous.

Science fiction has also traditionally believed in imperialism as an appropriate approach to other worlds and cultures. All alien societies encountered are seen as the other and as a threat, to be wiped out or deprived of autonomy. Not so for Merril. The first alien that Emma Tarbell's group encounters on Uller is responsible for her husband's death and is itself killed. She hates it and at first sides with the rest of the colony who want to destroy any other of the creatures that they meet. Jose Cabrini argues for a chance to study, and perhaps learn to communicate with the aliens, which eventually happens.

Merril's short novel is inspiring, energy-giving, and also hopeful. That is, within the context of male-female conflicts, the suggestion is that there are ways to integrate the sex roles that are more productive of human happiness than those we have now. In 1953, not many people, men or women, were questioning the validity of traditional sex roles, at least not in public. Merril was questioning, but her story suggests that there could be an accommodation between men and women. Though Judith Merril may or may not have believed in the myth that men protect and care for women, this myth did inform much of the consciousness of that decade and may explain the optimism in a work that in other ways is quite a rigorous refutation of traditional values.

Joanna Russ and James Tiptree, Jr., have no such illusions. "When It Changed" by Russ and "The Women Men Don't See" and "Houston, Houston, Do You Read?" by Tiptree take a curious but valid approach to a theme that has long been a mainstay of science fiction—the nature of the alien. One view has remained fairly constant in the genre—the alien is a threat, real or perceived, to earth dwellers or travelers, and must be dealt with on that level.

The difference is that the alien in Russ's and Tiptree's work is the human male. The threatened earthlings are women, a bleak and pessimistic metaphor for the current state of male-female relations. Yet many women who would not agree that it is appropriate practically would assent to its emotional rightness.

Tiptree's two stories have a male point of view, one a narrator, and one in the third person. Both characters are exposed to a view in which—as far as women are concerned—men are the major cause of pain and suffering. Both males are astonished to learn this fact, even as they are in the process of proving the women's point. In "Houston, Houston, Do You Read?" three male astronauts complete their orbit around the sun and proceed back to earth. In their attempts to reestablish contact with earth, from which comes the title of the story, they learn gradually and unbelievingly that they have encountered a time warp on the far side of the sun and have been launched 300 years into the future. Their ship, the *Sunbird*, has been listed in earth's history books as "lost . . .

never came back." The spaceship *Gloria,* piloted by women, rescues the men as their fuel is about to run out, and on the journey back to earth they learn slowly of the changes that have taken place since they left earth. They try, at first mutely, then with cunning, to adapt. But of course they cannot; the assumptions and attitudes with which they left earth as members of a dominant class cannot be transformed easily, if at all.

Tiptree handles this section with a fair amount of sympathy for the male characters, who have been deprived of their wives and families and all that is familiar to them. The women are kind and try to ease their pain, revealing the major changes slowly and protectively so as to spare the men as much future shock as possible. This is not wholly compassion on the women's part, but also a realistic approach to a species that their history books tell them was violent and destructive and believed totally in its own importance.

And major changes there have been! The world population has been reduced to about two million inhabitants by a global plague that has caused widespread sterility. The plague was most destructive to the Y-chromosome, which determines the male fetus, so that live births since the epidemic have all been female. Furthermore, reproduction is at present accomplished through cloning. Somatic cell nuclei are inserted in an enucleated ovum and implanted in the womb. Each clone daughter (the women refer to them as sisters) has a womb mother who nurses her for a time following birth. Then the children are given into the care of that portion of the population that has chosen mothering as an activity.

Each genotype, or clone strain, has a history book. On the space ship are two women, Judy Dakar and Judy Paris, from the original genotype of Judy Shapiro. As they explain to one of the men:

"We each have a book, it's really a library. All the recorded messages. The Book of Judy Shapiro, that's us. Dakar and Paris are our personal names. We're doing cities now." They laugh, trying not to talk at once about how each Judy adds her individual memoir, her adventures and problems and discoveries in the genotype they all share. "If you make a mistake, it's useful for the others . . . we make excerpts of the parts we like best. And practical things, like Judys should watch out for skin cancer."

Lorimer, from whose point of view we observe, is horrified. He is aghast that these women have succeeded in finding a humane and personal means of imposing control on genetic evolution. "I think it's sad," he says.

"But that's just what we think about you," the younger Judy bursts out. How do you know who you *are*? Or who anybody is? All alone, no sisters to share with! You don't know what you can do, or what would be interesting to try. All you poor singletons, you—why, you just have to blunder along and die, all for nothing . . ."

Later, Lorimer asks:

"What kind of songs do you sing?" "Oh, every kind. Adventure songs, work songs, mothering songs, roaming songs, mood songs, trouble songs, joke songs—everything."
    "What about love songs? Do you still have, well, love?"
    "Of course, how could people not love?" But she looks at him doubtfully. "The love stories I've heard from your times are so, I don't know, so weird. Grim and pluggy. It doesn't seem like love . . ."

After the men recover from their initial shock, they begin fantasizing about how they can capitalize on this new world in which they are the only three males. In a drunken monologue that even disgusts his male colleagues, Bud rhapsodizes, "Nothing but pussy everywhere. I can do anything I want, any time . . . They'll be spread out for miles begging for it . . . Hey, I'll have contests, only the best for old Buddy now."
    The religious male, Dave, has a different approach. "They are lost children. They have forgotten He who made them.

For generations they have lived in darkness. . . . Help me to teach the children Thy holy law and train them in the fear of Thy righteous wrath. Let the women learn in silence and all subjection. . . . They shall have sons to rule over them and glorify Thy name." Bud eventually rapes one of the women and Dave pulls his gun to try to take over the ship "in the name of the United States of America under God."

Lorimer, the narrator, tries to tell the women that these are good men who have been pushed to the breaking point. When he tries to justify their behavior by saying that everybody has aggressive fantasies, he is told quietly and without apology by the women that *they* don't. He then tries to point out all the good men have done for women over the centuries, building civilizations, protecting women and children. "We protected you, we worked our balls off keeping you and your kids. It was hard. It was a fight, a bloody fight all the way. We're tough. We had to be, can't you understand?"

The ship's captain, Lady Blue, replies:

"We are trying, Dr. Lorimer. But you must see there's a problem. As I understand it, what you protected people from was largely other males, wasn't it? But the fighting is long over. It ended when you did, I believe. We can hardly turn you loose on Earth and we simply have no facilities for people with your emotional problems."

" 'Your problem is,' " Lorimer says, " 'if you could take the risk of giving us equal rights, what could we possibly contribute?' " " 'Precisely,' says Lady Blue." The climax is appropriate, necessary, and unapologetic.

"Houston, Houston . . .", demonstrates Tiptree's skill as a writer. In one short story, she manages to stay in control of several elements—the unfolding of the new world the women have made and their joy in and with it, the alternating attraction of the men for the women versus the horror at what they are learning, and the changing feelings on the part of the reader between sympathy for the men in the time warp and disgust at their reversion to aggressive behavior. Tiptree veers from absurdity to panic to dry description in the space of a paragraph.

In the second of Tiptree's stories, "The Women Men Don't See," the theme of human male as alien is seen in the context of a plot that includes an outer space being as a second, a real alien, in terms of most of science fiction.

The male narrator is Don Fenton, one of three tourists whose plane crashes into a sandbar in a mangrove swamp on the Yucatan Peninsula. Ruth Parsons and her daughter Althea are the other passengers: Esteban, a Mayan, is the pilot. Fenton is an intelligence agent, probably CIA, on a fishing trip, who carries a hefty amount of paranoia around with him like extra luggage. Parsons is a clerk for the CIA; she and her daughter are on a tour of Mayan sites.

When the plane goes down, Fenton and Ruth Parsons walk across the sandbar to find fresh water. While he asks himself sexual and political questions about her, she keeps him at arm's length, both physically and emotionally. And she reveals only enough about herself to maintain a social relationship with him. His paranoia about who she is and what harm she may mean to him and how he could ward off that harm by confronting her sexually are all well described. The situation becomes a workable metaphor for many situations in which men must deal with women on a level other than equal to equal.

What Parsons has against Fenton, of course, is that he's male and therefore an alien. She watches him closely because to Tiptree women need to watch men closely, not because she has any CIA-oriented designs on him. Her previous involvement with a man has been to get pregnant; she did not marry him. She was apparently conceived and raised in the same way, and there is a suggestion that she has left her daughter with the pilot in order to let *her* get pregnant. She chose the Mayan because he is a type (genetic) of person she thinks highly of. So, childbearing is important, and choosing good genes, too, but no involvement on a human level, not with men. At one point she says to the narrator,

" 'Oh, there wasn't any trauma, Don, and I don't *hate* men. That would be as silly as—as hating the weather . . .' "

Parsons scoffs at women's liberation as a doomed venture and predicts that in a real crisis, any rights or progress gained by women will swiftly disappear. When Fenton tries to assure her that we're all in this together, men and women alike, she casually points out that the degree of power held by each makes all the difference in the world: " 'Men hate wars, too, Ruth,' I say as gently as I can. 'I know,' she shrugs and climbs to her feet. 'But that's your problem, isn't it?' "

Into this situation come real aliens, from somewhere out in the galaxy. Ruth convinces them to take her and her daughter with them wherever they plan to go. When they communicate to her that they have no plans to return to earth for a long time, if ever, she says, " 'We don't want to come back. Please take us with you.' "

The narrator's paranoia is replaced by a sense of unreality, that any woman could "go sight unseen to an alien world . . . Is that some system of upbringing?" But Parsons says " '*We survive by ones and twos in the chinks of your world-machine . . . I'm used to aliens.*' "

Joanna Russ's story "When It Changed" has a female narrator, Janet, resident of Whileaway, a colony of earth people somewhere in space, whose men all died out shortly after the colony was settled. Women are now married to women and bear children by the process of ovum-sharing. Janet and Katy have a daughter, Yuki. The women are technologically competent and for the most part happy and productive. There are, though, a couple of suggestions of dueling and intense rivalries, so everything is not peaceful.

Enter the aliens, the first earthmen to land on Whileaway for thirty generations. They admire what the women have done but fail to understand why they, the men, are not welcomed with open arms. After all, now the women can be protected and cared for again. Now they can have a complete life, a woman's society being only half-complete, and so forth. " 'A great tragedy,' " says one man when informed of the death of the males thirty generations ago. " 'Yes, a great tragedy. But it's over.' And again he looked around at all of us with the strangest deference. As if we were invalids." As in the two stories by Tiptree, the description of any given male who sees a situation in which his absence is not cause for comment, if not grief, is both humorous and enraging, and very, very real.

In a touch of humor among the tears. Janet asks her daughter, " 'Yuki, do you think you could fall in love with a man?' and she whooped derisively. 'With a ten foot toad!' said her tactful child." Of course, the women on Whileaway will lose. There are few of them and they aren't war-oriented. There are many men still on earth. They want these women, need them genetically. If the women don't welcome this state of affairs, well that's hard for the men to understand, but the women will comply. The narrator sits alone at the close of the story and mourns for the impending loss of a world that she loved.

"Building Block" by Sondra Dorman is in many ways a traditional story. It is different in that its protagonist has characteristics that are rarely allowed to women. The story looks at a world that resembles our own in many recognizable ways. There are rich and poor, and the poor are isolated physically in ghettoes; money, called credits, is a god and must be paid before goods or services are returned, and personal and business relationships are often cutthroat.

In this future world people live in individual space houses, many of which are designed and built by the woman, Norja, who owns Sky Castles, Inc. Norja, the architect-business-woman narrator of the story, is currently suffering from too much liquor and a creative block in her work. She is rapidly approaching bankruptcy, after which she envisions living in the poverty area. She has misplaced, both physically and in her mind, the plans for a new building concept that she feels sure will revolutionize space architecture and incidentally get her back on solid financial footing.

Desperate for her sanity and her reputation (her spider-web like structures have earned her the respect of clients and competitors—they call her Arachne), Norja consults two therapists, one an old friend of the family, who give her memory drugs to enable her to recapture her vision. They both betray her. In each case when she awakens from the drug, having spilled her blueprints from her subconscious into a tape recorder, they tell her they are holding the tape for ransom; she can either pay them off or they will sell her plans to her biggest competitors.

Alternating between depression and rage, Norja fantasizes herself living in poverty with the other poor. But she redeems the situation. Out of desperation she starts creating and soon has the plans for a space building project that will house the poor for less than they pay now, provide beautiful surroundings, and incidentally make a lot of money for herself and for whoever takes on the building contract.

Norja is every architect who has had to make the leap from individual family structures to mass housing. She is also every protagonist who has suffered from creative block and the conflict between artistic risk and business security, except that the latter have, in American fiction, almost without exception been men. Norja, a woman character taking an artistic and business risk, is something daring in itself.

In the process of convincing hard-nosed businessmen of the value of her vision, she experiences more cold feet, then plunges ahead, because what does she have to lose, how more broke can you be than broke? "This is how you make a living, remember? You run out on the rope and never mind the other end, because the rope is you, and you'll fasten it when you get there."

The five works dealt with in this essay have considered a handful of major feminist themes: 1) the importance of daughters as makers and interpreters of history, 2) the success of worlds run completely or at least equally, by women, 3) the human male as an alien form, and 4) the importance of the individual woman creator. These same works, in a variety of combinations, also consider other important themes, although in a less intense and detailed way.

Russ's story and Tiptree's "Houston, Houston . . ." consider female homosexuality as a valid way of loving, reproducing, and running a society. Other science fiction has begun to talk about a more liberating sexuality, but lesbianism is still not portrayed very often or positively in any literature. In both stories, the description of the nature of love between women has elements of what we know as romance, that is, it is highly idealistic, sexual, and demanding.

It differs from Western romantic concepts, however, in that lovers are equals, not unfinished and missing halves of each other. They do important work including childbearing, and, at least in the case of "Houston, Houston . . ." they don't combine feelings of sexual romance with those of hostility and jealousy.

Some of Russ's characters, however, fight duels, apparently over each other, and kill wild animals as a test of adulthood.

Women as competent technicians, scientists, or artists is a theme running through several of the works—notably *Daughters of Earth,* "When It Changed," "Houston, Houston, Do You Read?" and "Building Block." In *Daughters,* Joan Thurman, the first voyager daughter, theorizes and perfects the TAP—the Thurman Atmospheric Process, which leads to the building of the first open-air city on Pluto. Emma, her granddaughter, is a doctor and a scientist, whose work leads to breaking the code and establishing communication with the aliens on Uller. Leah, Emma's daughter, studies her mother's work and becomes a spokeswoman for convincing the rest of the colony that the Ullerns should be equal partners with the humans in any future space ventures.

In Russ's "When It Changed," the technological competence of the women has been assured before the story begins. Both men and women sent to Whileaway have been picked because they were two or three experts in one—in the areas of mechanics, radio operations, industrial techniques, and farming methods. And since the men have all died, the women have become technically expert at reproducing through ovum-sharing.

In Tiptree's "Houston, Houston . . . ," the women who now

rule earth have chosen five basic activities out of the hundreds that were common before the plague. They concentrate their scientific skills on food (farming and fishing), communications, transport (includng space travel, which they have perfected), factories for production of goods, and reproduction, which consists of cloning.

In "Building Block," Norja is both a competent artist and businesswoman whose commitment to both of these disciplines is endangered by the greed of people with less character, as well as the nature of the economic system. While many fictional women derive their strength and identity through a commitment to family or other persons, Norja's strength and inspiration come from within, from her devotion to a professional and a personal discipline.

Another theme handled almost casually in both *Daughters of Earth* and "Houston, Houston . . ." is that of ethnic diversity. Both works conceive of new societies that contain beings other than white Western derivatives. In "Houston, Houston . . . ," the genotypes from which the population is reproduced include representatives of all the major races and several of the minor ones. One main character is black, another of Caribbean extraction. In *Daughters*, the diversity is made up mostly of whites, but the inclusion of Jewish, Polish, and Italian names was a step up in the Fifties.

The quality of the emotional atmosphere in which the major characters live should be remarked on. Norja, in Dorman's "Building Block," creates in more of an emotional vacuum than the characters in the other works. Merril's daughters have family and professional support. Tiptree's sisters (in "Houston, Houston . . .") have each other, as do Russ's women in "When It Changed." Norja is pretty much of a loner, both professionally and emotionally, though she has a colleague-assistant who believes in her.

The works considered in this essay vary widely between optimism and pessimism with regard to women's life in the future. Merril's and Dorman's works suggest that women will be strong, competent, and risk-taking in company with men, or at least in a social order where men are numerous, although the women will have some of the same problems that we do today. Tiptree and Russ suggest that women will be all right as long as men are eliminated or, in the case of "The Women Men Don't See," that they surely won't be all right as long as men rule.

This question of male absence is important. Is it coincidence that in both stories "Houston, Houston . . ." and "When It Changed" the men have disappeared through an act of God, or at least not by an act of women? The women have not had to revolt, go to war, or anything else that has them directly confront male power. Both concentrate on the kind of society women will build on their own, after the elimination of males.

In some ways, Dorman's story is the most traditional of the five, in that it concentrates on the importance of the individual artistic struggle amidst the greed of society and individuals. The difference is that the role of the traditional isolated artist male hero has been turned into a woman. But a large section of current feminist vision is looking beyond the individual, to a social order that is less alienated and more collective, along the lines of those women seen in *Daughters of Earth*, "Houston, Houston . . . ," and "When It Changed."

It is clear that the coming years will see a great deal more science fiction written by women. They will expand on the themes spoken of in this essay and they will probe others. It is possible that this genre, in a source founded by a woman, may become a more congenial place for women, both as writers and as readers.

6

Lucy Menger

THE APPEAL OF
CHILDHOOD'S END

Arthur C. Clarke's *Childhood's End* is a peculiar novel. It has no hero or heroine. The story is a series of loosely connected episodes. The plot is austere. The core themes in the book are conflicting and that conflict is never resolved.

These hardly sound like the specifications for a successful book. Nevertheless, *Childhood's End* is perhaps the most successful of Clarke's many writings. First published in the United States in August of 1953, it has gone through thirty-eight printings, the most recent in December of 1977.

Few books in any literary genre maintain popularity over a quarter of a century. Why has a book as peculiar as *Childhood's End* done so?

This question has no easy answer. *Childhood's End* is the sum of many parts. Plot, story, themes, characters, Clarke's felicitious writing style, subtlety, and humor all work together. Moreover, the linearity of Clarke's narrative mode is deceptive. *Childhood's End* is a carefully built structure with theme, episode, and character doing double, sometimes triple, duty to give the book unity and substance. In some ways, then, *Childhood's End* is more than the sum of its parts.

The plot has mythic simplicity and force: Under the guardianship of aliens, humankind gives birth to its successor race and then dies. Clarke's is no parochial view. His "childhood's end" is not the end of the childhood of the human race.

Instead, it is a stage in the evolution of a chain of life in which homo sapiens is only one link. Clarke's Last Man ponders the mighty entity that mankind has spawned and, with resignation, muses: This was "an end that repudiated optimism and pessimism alike. Yet it was fitting: it had the sublime inevitability of a great work of art."

Not an easy acceptance to which to lead a reader. Yet this is exactly what Clarke does with hint and bait and legerdemain. This feat of persuasion is surely one of the reasons for *Childhood's End*'s continuing popularity.

Childhood's End opens with an ending. The coming of a people from the stars, named the Overlords by men, stops the American and Russian race to be the first in space with nuclear rockets. The Overlords remain hidden in their starships. They take over the United Nations as their administrative arm on earth and the only man who has personal contact with them is Rikki Stormgren, Secretary-General of the U. N. Even Stormgren never sees an Overlord. His contact is limited to conversations with Karellen, the Overlord Supervisor of Earth.

After five years of Overlord stewardship, earth is at peace. Nonetheless, some resent and fear the Overlords. Others, like Stormgren, though convinced of the Overlords' good intentions toward mankind, are troubled by their refusal to show themselves.

Stormgren is kidnapped by radicals who intend to defy the Overlords' suzerainty. He is kept in a deserted mine until the leaders of the radical group assemble to question him about his contacts with Karellen. In the midst of this interrogation, Stormgren is rescued by the Overlords. Karellen later admits to Stormgren that he had been used as bait to draw the radical leaders into the open. Piqued at being used in this way, Stormgren, who is about to retire as Secretary-General, determines to find out, if he can, what the Overlords look like.

Shortly after the kidnapping, Karellen tells Stormgren that the Overlords will show themselves to mankind in fifty years.

At his final meeting with Karellen, Stormgren makes his attempt to discover what the Overlords look like. He succeeds partially, but never reveals what he has seen. He realizes that the Overlords had judged correctly in keeping themselves hidden.

A lapse of fifty years occurs. The narrative reopens on the day the Overlords are to reveal themselves. Karellen descends from his ship. He looks exactly like a devil, complete with leathery wings and barbed tail. Mankind is shocked but, after fifty-five years of peace and diminishing ignorance, has enough stability that the trauma caused by the Overlord's appearance soon passes.

Under the Overlords, Earth experiences a Golden Age. The world is one nation, with few areas not within easy reach by air car. Ignorance and illness have dwindled and prosperity is general. The Overlords continue to supervise earth. They tell little of themselves, but walk among men and study mankind.

Nonetheless, George Greggson, a stage designer, is surprised to discover an Overlord studying a friend's extensive library on psychic matters. He is, moreover, embarrassed when this Overlord watches the operation of a sophisticated Ouija board. George, his date Jean Morrel, and others are at the board. As the session is about to end, a watcher, Jan Rodericks, asks which star is the Overlords' sun. The board answers with a series of numbers and letters. Jean Morrel faints and the session breaks up.

Jan, who wants to go into space, discovers that the Ouija's letters and numbers designate a star that is in the direction taken by the Overlords' supply ships.

With help, Jan stows away on one of the supply ships. The Overlords' ships travel at near the speed of light, so Jan knows the ship, he, and the other passengers will experience only a few months en route while decades are passing on earth. Nevertheless, he sleeps the trip away in drug-induced hibernation.

Meanwhile, back on the planet, the Overlords keep watch on

Jean, now married to George Greggson, and on their two children, Jeff and Poppet. Jeff starts to have strange dreams in which he travels to distant planets. George goes to the Overlords, whom he knows have been watching Jeff, and asks for an explanation. He is told that Jeff is not human and that shortly the rest of the children of earth will become like Jeff. When this transformation occurs, the Overlords reveal their reason for coming to Earth. They came to shepherd the human race through this metamorphosis, a metamorphosis which will meld the children of man into an entity. When sufficiently mature, this entity will join other entities like it.

The Overlords take the children to an area where they can develop without interference or threat from human beings. As the children evolve, the human race dies.

When Jan returns from the Overlords' planet, Karellen tells him what has happened. Jan is the last human alive. The Overlords warn Jan that they don't know what the entity the children have become will do to the earth. But he chooses to remain when, after a few years, the Overlords retreat to the edge of the solar system.

Finally the entity which had been the children leaves for the stars, dissolving the planet Earth as it does so. Their task complete, the Overlords return to their planet.

The above is a starved outline of Clarke's story. As it suggests, each individual episode is almost wholly independent. To weld them into a unit, Clarke uses a number of devices. One of these is the plot: It provides a single thread linking first page to last. Another is a web of suspense. Clarke keeps the reader wondering: What has happened? What is happening? What is going to happen?

The clarity of Clarke's writing style is misleading. He is a master at keeping the reader from knowing what is going on. In Chapter 1 (the Prologue), the Overlords' ships arrive, "huge and silent shadows driving across the stars. . . ." A rocket scientist recognizes that these must be alien ships and the chapter ends:

Only one thought echoed and re-echoed through Reinhold's brain:

The human race was no longer alone.

Chapter 2 picks up the story five years later with protest marchers approaching the United Nations building in New York. Clarke gives no clue as to what went on in the interim. He makes the reader wait to find out about the first contact with the Overlords and what has been happening since then. Before he gives these answers, however, he introduces other mysteries. What do the Overlords look like? Why won't they show themselves? What are their motivations in coming to earth? Judging by their actions, the Overlords' intentions toward the human race are good; but is this really true? Even if their intentions *are* good, do they know what *is* good for mankind?

Some of these questions Clarke answers early on. Others he does not. The questions relating to the Overlords' physical appearance are answered in Chapter 5. The Overlords' reasons for visiting earth are not disclosed until Chapter 20. As for the Overlords' beneficence, it is revealed bit by bit. However, this beneficence is not what the reader is likely to expect. It is the beneficence of a doctor with a dying patient. The Overlords do what they have to do in as humane a way as possible, while trying to learn as much about mankind as they can. Their objectives are mixed and the nature and reasons for the mixture do not become clear until the closing pages of the novel.

Clarke keeps suspense building and interweaving throughout *Childhood's End*. On first reading, this suspense is the primary device that holds the novel together. On subsequent readings—and *Childhood's End* greatly rewards re-reading—the contribution of other elements to the unity and appeal of the book become more evident. One such binding element is Clarke's use of themes.

Two opposed themes dominate his novel. The first of these is the power of reason: the omnipotence of rational thought.

In the first third of *Childhood's End*, Clarke firmly establishes the potency of intellect and reason. The Overlords are the epitome of intellect—Karellen demonstrates "overwhelming intellectual power"—and their "mastery of the physical universe" is the logical outcome of that intellect. Without violence, by judicious use of their power, the Overlords put an end to war and organized cruelty and bring prosperity to the world. Compared to the Overlords, humans are not so much children as mental dwarfs.

By the end of Chapter 6, Clarke has made a strong case for the supremacy of the rational mind and has probably also seduced the reader into believing that the remainder of *Childhood's End* will be an elaboration of this theme. He then, however, introduces his second major theme: the power of the irrational. This theme revolves around abilities that even the Overlords' mighty minds cannot comprehend: the transcendent power of paraphysics, that cluster of abilities lumped together as "extra sensory perception" or "psi"—astral travel, clairvoyance, telepathy, and telekinesis.

The tension generated by the conflict between these two themes dominates the final two-thirds of *Childhood's End*. In the first third of his novel, Clarke has shown the Overlords to be reason incarnate. Their interest in earth and mankind seems anomalous. Why all this concern?

The second theme provides the answer to this question, but as usual Clarke doesn't hurry to make this clear. Again, he keeps the reader wondering. He hints. The first hint is an Overlord reading an entire library wholly devoted to psychic matters. Temporarily, this is dismissed with the comment: "Surely you'd study the superstitions of any primitive race you were having dealings with!"

The hints grow stronger. A sophisticated Ouija board produces the catalogue number of the star that is the Overlords' sun. Shortly thereafter the Overlords identify Jean Morrel, who had been assisting with the Ouija board, as the probable source of this star number. They decide she must be closely related to the "Prime Contact." Clarke, of course, gives no clue as to prime contact with what.

At this point in the narrative, Clarke leaves Jean in George Greggson's dubious care and turns to the first installment of Jan Rodericks's adventures.

Paraphysics fades into the background. Once Jan has discovered that the number produced by the Ouija board is almost certainly that of the Overlords' sun, psychic matters are scarcely mentioned until Jan is safely tucked away aboard an Overlord ship, sleeping his way to the stars.

Clarke drops the subject of paraphysics into the story like a seed in fertile ground. Having done so and moved on does not mean that he has discarded the subject. Though hidden, its influence is present and growing. The final episodes of *Childhood's End* turn on the incident at the Ouija board. George marries Jean and fathers the Prime Contact because his experience with the Ouija board has undercut his rejection of Jean's interest in psychic matters. And Jan, who has been drifting, is galvanized by possession of the knowledge of which star is the Overlords' sun. Given the opportunity, he knows he could travel on an Overlord starship to their sun and back in his lifetime.

Clarke's second theme can remain latent only so long. Psychic matters return to the narrative when Jeff, George and Jean's son, starts having "dreams." George says of these dreams:

> I never believed that they were simply the imaginings of a child. They were so incredible that—I know this sounds ridiculous—they had to be based on some reality.

George is correct. Jeff is traveling mentally to ever more distant star systems.

From this point on in Clarke's narrative, the theme relating to psychic power becomes increasingly dominant.

Clarke is facing his reader with a mighty question. Can psychic power, which is so contrary to the logic of science, be, in fact, a reasonable and logical occurrence?

Although he appears to do so, Clarke never answers this question. His "answer" is a matter of logic. By definition, psychic phenomena are irrational because they violate the known laws of the universe. Yet, in discussing Jeff's dream travels, George Greggson and an Overlord have the following conversation. George speaks first.

> "I've never believed in the supernatural: I'm not a scientist, but I think there's a rational explanation for everything."
> "There is," said Rashaverak.

Rashaverak, the Overlord, is saying that psychic phenomena do have a rational explanation. Yet, by its nature reason cannot lead to an understanding of the irrational. It can only lead to an understanding of rational matters. Therefore, if, as Rashaverak affirms, psychic phenomena have a rational explanation, they are rational and not essentially different from reason. In such a circumstance, psychic power would simply be a stronger power than reason, more effective and more efficient. The thematic conflict would, then, be illusory. Psychic power and reason would be members of the same hierarchy, with psychic power several notches higher. There would be no more conflict between Clarke's themes than between the first and second string of a football team.

To his credit, Clarke doesn't pander to his readers with such a safe, pat answer. Instead, he hints and whispers and finally states that reason is not an unfailing tool. There is so much that his paragons of reason, the Overlords, don't understand. Rashaverak refers to the metamorphosis of the children:

> "I will not deceive you. We can study and observe, as we are doing already. But we cannot interfere, because we cannot understand."

Karellen speaks on why the Overlords came to earth:

> "I cannot explain the full nature of the threat you represented. It would not have been a threat to us, and therefore we do not comprehend it."

Again Karellen speaks, this time of humanity's psychic abilities:

> "All these potentialities, all these latent powers—we do not possess them, nor do we understand them. Our intellects are far more powerful than yours, but there is something in your minds that has always eluded us."

Rashaverak's statement that there is a rational explanation for everything is, clearly, a tenet of faith. He and his people cannot understand either mankind or their own master, the Overmind. How can he be so sure there are "rational explanations" for either, much less for "everything?"

Having insinuated the idea into the reader's mind that the universe may be too much for the reasoning powers of either man or Overlord, Clarke wisely does not try to resolve the unresolvable. Reason exists and is effective within a given sphere. Psychic powers also exist and are even more effective in a larger sphere. He leaves it at that. He leaves the reader to make his own decision.

One of the pleasures of *Childhood's End* is that Clarke does give the reader so much to consider. The major themes, discussed above, concern important questions that merit much reflection.

These are not the only questions worth pondering in *Childhood's End*, however. There are many. Clarke's answers, though never the only possible ones, are generally satisfying.

What would a super race be like? According to Clarke, they would be quite admirable. His Overlords are not only intellectually brilliant, they are also kind, just, and merciful. Clarke leaves many questions about them unanswered, however. Their biological background, the structure of their society, their individual motivations (if any), their relationships with each other are touched on only glancingly.

Clarke is more generous in his answers to how a near-term Utopia might be established and what it would be like. The underpinning for his Utopia is, of course, the Overlords.

Yet what the Overlords accomplish—the cessation of war and the establishment of a world state—though unlikely in the immediate future, is not beyond the power of men to achieve. Peace and a global nation free facilities once used to manufacture war materials. The result is a cornucopia of consumer goods. The citizens of the world have ample material wealth and the leisure to enjoy it, as computer management of production virtually eliminates the drudgery that had bowed mankind for ages.

In Clarke's Utopia, his Golden Age, humans do work worthy of the human brain. This results in a flowering of human activity, but without great achievement. A worm lurks in the apple.

> There were drawbacks, of course, though they were willingly accepted. One had to be very old indeed to realize that the papers which the telecaster printed in every home were really rather dull. Gone were the crises that had once produced banner headlines. There were no mysterious murders to baffle the police and to arouse in a million breasts the moral indignation that was often suppressed envy.

Boredom is the drowsing demon of Clarke's Utopia.

Clarke proposes still another possibility chilling to the rampant human ego. Is mankind equal to the stars?

> "In this galaxy of ours," murmured Karellen, "there are eighty seven thousand million suns. Even that figure gives only a faint idea of the immensity of space. In challenging it, you would be like ants attempting to level and classify all the grains of sand in all the deserts of the world."

Clarke, the astronomer, is speaking. If his implied verdict is correct, what frontiers remain open to the human, the incorrigible adventurer?

Clarke's characters handle individual questions in individual ways. Stormgren copes with the challenge of the Overlords' enormous superiority by sticking to his ideals of service to man. George handles the same challenge by turning away from society at large and joining a community dedicated to the elaboration of a specifically and defiantly terrestrial culture. When the opportunity arrives, Jan chooses risk instead of safety and stultification. By permitting different characters to meet various challenges in their own ways, Clarke has avoided burdening his novel with the albatross of a stereotypic superhero who grapples resolutely with all challenges.

Having a series of characters does, however, deprive Clarke of a thread that helps to hold most novels together: continuous reader interest in, and sympathetic involvement with, one hero (or heroine) and that character's experiences.

Clarke's delineation of his characters is also uneven. Karellen and Stormgren are the strongest portrayals. Karellen, Supervisor of Earth, is the only principal who survives from the beginning to the end of *Childhood's End*. His participation in the story is intermittent, however. On first reading, Clarke's portrait of Karellen is only provocative; on subsequent readings, the bits of characterization strewn throughout the novel cohere and Clarke's portrait gains stature. Karellen compels sympathy.

Creating a sympathetic alien is no easy task. To be convincing and satisfying to a reader, an alien must differ from the human mode in mind even more than in body. A man in a monster suit won't do. Yet at the same time, an alien must possess enough human traits to allow human readers to understand and empathize with him (her) (it). Karellen meets these specifications. He, like the other Overlords, is virtually immortal and therefore is without the impatiences and fears that mortality breeds. There is no evidence that he is a sexual being. He seems to lack the emotionality of mankind, yet he is not without feelings. Karellen feels pity. He is kind. He tempers his actions with mercy. Stormgren is sure that Karellen is truly his friend. Still, Karellen remains essentially nonhuman. Knowing his race's ambitions to be unattainable, he also knows "they would hold fast until the end: they would await whatever destiny was theirs." The dignity with which the Overlords' pathetic pursuit of the impossible is conducted is moving; it is, nonetheless, inhuman.

Stormgren, like Karellen, has dignity, but he is very much a human and a likeable one. He is self-aware. He has a sense of humor. He takes his objectives, but not himself, seriously. When circumstance requires, he can relax. Stormgren is doped, kidnapped, and hidden in a deserted mine. When he regains consciousness, he discovers that his jailers are eager to play poker with him while waiting for their superiors to arrive. Stormgren is the number one man in the Overlords' administration of earth: In effect, he is the president of Earth. Yet, realizing his total helplessness, he sits down to play poker and does so with enthusiasm.

Stormgren knows when to speak and when to keep quiet. After he glimpses Karellen, he keeps what he has seen a secret for over thirty years.

Though able and courageous, Stormgren is essentially a humble individual. He is sure of Karellen's affection for him and "though it might be the affection of a man for a devoted and intelligent dog, it was none the less sincere for that, and Stromgren's life had given him few greater satisfactions."

George Greggson does not have Stormgren's strength either as a person or as a portrait. Nevertheless, he grows in depth and becomes more sympathetic as the narrative progresses. George enters the story as a womanizer with Jean Morrel his current favorite—perhaps. He is not merely a womanizer; he is also somewhat of a stuffed shirt. When, startled at unexpectedly meeting an Overlord, Jean chatters inanely, he comments: "Really, darling! You just *don't* talk to Overlords that way!" And he is contemptuous of Jean's interest in psychic matters.

Although George is querulous and self-centered, he is not all bad. When the presence of an Overlord overshadows a bride's introduction to her husband's friends, George feels sympathy for her: It should have been her day. He is awed into sobriety by the beauty of the African landscape. When Jean faints at the Ouija board, he feels tenderness for her and accepts his feelings for what they are.

George has the courage to face not only his pleasant feelings, but also his fears. "The universe was vast, but that fact terrified him less than its mystery. . . . He had no wish to face whatever lurked in the unknown darkness, just beyond the little circle of light cast by the lamp of Science." He recognizes the mystery and, if he chooses to turn his back on it, this act has the dignity of a conscious decision.

When mystery enters his own life, however, George doesn't turn away. His son, Jeff, reports being saved from danger by a voice and the dissolving of a boulder. George doesn't reject this story as a child's fantasy. Instead, he investigates and accepts what he finds as confirming his son's strange story. Later when Jeff's dream travels begin and Poppet, Jeff's sister, develops psychic powers, George doesn't temporize. He goes directly to the Overlords for explanation and help. To his sorrow, they have none to give.

Jan Rodericks, like George, has courage. His, however, is not the courage of a realist but of a romantic. In Clarke's *Golden Age*, disease has been virtually wiped out and longevity increased. Lengthened life and a vanishing need for unskilled labor have led to prolonged education. At 27, Jan is still a college boy with years of education ahead of him.

Jan longs to go into space. As the Overlords have the only space vehicles and don't lend out their sophisticated hardware, his longing is more of a pipedream than an ambition. With the path of his dream blocked, Jan is marking time. A whole lifetime of marking time seems to lie ahead of him.

Jan is the watcher who asks the Ouija board which star is the Overlords' sun. To ask such a question in the presence of an Overlord, as Jan did, is perhaps a measure of his need for something at least bordering on adventure. It is a small gesture, but nonetheless a gesture, of defiance. More notably, in interrogating the Ouija board, Jan displays a willingness to turn away from the rational, because the rational world of the Overlords has failed him. This marks him as a very different person from George, who expresses his rebellion in work.

Jan also differs significantly from George in his reaction to the knowledge he has gained via the Ouija board. George is uneasy with events that are out of the ordinary and does his best to ignore them. Jan ignores the source and accepts the datum. His reaction to discovering that the number spelled by the Ouija board designated a star in the direction taken by the Overlords' homebound ships was:

> It was an impossible coincidence. NGS 549672 *must* be the home of the Overlords. Yet to accept the fact violated all Jan's cherished ideas of scientific method. Very well—let them be violated. He must accept the fact that, somehow, Rupert's fantastic experiment had tapped a hitherto unknown source of knowledge.

Ironically, in his acceptance of what he has discovered, Jan is not being "unscientific." He is, rather, acting in the best traditions of science. When an honest scientist's beliefs conflict with evidence, the beliefs, not the evidence, must be jettisoned. This is exactly what Jan does.

Jan may be a romantic, but he is also a pragmatist. He uses the knowledge he has come by to calculate the length of the journey to the Overlords' star and so finds that this journey is not too long for him to take—if he can board an Overlord ship. When the chance to stow away comes, Jan takes it.

> What finally decided him was the thought that, if he neglected this incredible opportunity, he would never forgive himself. All the rest of his life would be spent in vain regrets—and nothing could be worse than that.

Jan gets his adventure and, in the adventuring, learns his limits and becomes a man. Jan the boy becomes Jan the man and, in the final pages of *Childhood's End,* he becomes Clarke's voice of man musing on the fate of his race.

Clarke's portrait of Jean Morrel, wife of George and mother of Jeff and Poppet, is much less fully drawn than are those of his male characters. Except for her psychic powers, Jean never escapes from stereotype and a rather insipid stereotype at that. She is jealous of George's admiration of another woman. She gossips with other women about other women. When she marries George, she becomes a dutiful loving wife whose life is centered on her children. As she and George are investigating a new home, Jean thinks: "And the children would love it. That, in the final analysis, was all that mattered." Rather a narrow area of concern: It is not too surprising that Jean's George has a Carolle on the side. In the narrative, Jean's function scarcely exceeds that of psychic uterus: She has to be there to give birth to the Prime Contact. Moreover, not only is her individuality undefined; so is her role in society. George works. What Jean does with her time in an era of ubiquitous labor-saving devices and catered meals remains a mystery.

If Jean is a weakness in Clarke's novel, his sketches of minor characters are a strength. In the Prologue, the two rocket scientists come quickly to life. Thirty years before the era when the novel opens, both had worked for the Nazis at Peenemunde. As World War II wound down, they had defected, but to different sides. Schneider went to Russia, Hoffmann to the U.S. Each rose to head the nuclear rocket development program in his adopted homeland. Each respects the other and each wonders whether the other will win the race for space. Despite their surface similarities, Clarke makes clear that these men are dissimilar. The way he does so tells much about their characters.

When the Overlords' starships arrive, Schneider looks out the window and sees them—"and for the first time in his life he knew despair."

Hoffmann, too, sees the starships, but he "felt no regrets as the work of a lifetime was swept away. He had labored to take man to the stars, and, in the moment of success, the stars—the aloof, indifferent stars—had come to him."

Joe, Stormgren's jailer and poker opponent, is very different from Schneider and Hoffmann. Joe is a rebel who has found his cause in opposing the Overlords. He enjoys cloak-and-dagger operations and his pleasure in explaining to Stormgren how he was kidnapped is intense.

Joe comes to life through Stormgren's eyes. Joe is no mercenary, but Stormgren realizes "he had never thought seriously about the causes for which he was fighting. Emotion and extreme conservatism clouded all his judgements." The poker games are accompanied by an obbligato of political arguments. Though Joe reminds Stormgren of an "overgrown baby," he nevertheless feels that "when his [Joe's] type vanished, if it ever did, the world would be a safer but less interesting place." In Clarke's hands, Joe not only discloses his own character, but reveals much about Stormgren.

That Clarke himself is a scientist makes his delineation of Professor Sullivan, the ichthyologist, particularly interesting to contemplate. Sullivan provides Jan with aid and the means of defying the Overlords' ban on space travel for men. Other men may have been discouraged from scientific endeavors by the Overlords' superiority: not Sullivan. He risks his life to catalogue the living creatures of the ocean, and the possibility (even likelihood) that the Overlords could do the same job more easily and efficiently doesn't appear to deter him for a moment. He wants to study ocean life. Whether someone else might do this better is beside the point.

Sullivan's love of his work is what links him to Jan with his longing to go to the stars. Seeking Sullivan's aid, Jan asks what Sullivan would do if the Overlords would not let him near an ocean and he suddenly got a chance to achieve his goal. Jan asks: "Would you take the opportunity?"

Sullivan never hesitated.
"Of course. And argue later."

Clarke's Sullivan is a contented and self-directed man. He is also about as close to being proof against Utopia's boredom as is any human in *Childhood's End*.

The passing parade of varied personalities is certainly one of the pleasures of *Childhood's End*. However, despite their differences, Clarke's portraits all have one thing in common: His people are decent. They are kind and well-intentioned and their failings are very human weaknesses. No malice here. The acrid odor of evil is wholly absent from *Childhood's End*.

This absence of evil is, without doubt, one of the appeals of *Childhood's End*. To use a term that is perhaps unfashionable but that, hopefully, is not obsolete, *Childhood's End* is a wholesome book.

Childhood's End is shot through with suggestion and subtlety. In the Prologue, Clarke tells quite exactly what is going to occur in the novel's finale. This is hardly "giving away the plot," however, as the first time reader will not understand the message.

> This was the moment when history held its breath, and the present sheared asunder from the past as an iceberg splits from its frozen, parent cliffs, and goes sailing out to sea in lonely pride.

A better analogy of the death of the human race and the departure of the entity that had been its children is difficult to imagine.

With this analogy, Clarke has, in the Prologue, begun to prepare the reader for the denouement of his novel. Because of this preparation, when the denouement does occur, there is something familiar and inevitable about it. The reader recognizes what is happening without, perhaps, being able to place the source of his recognition.

This analogy does service in still another way. It points up a second parallel between the beginning and the conclusion of *Childhood's End.* The novel begins with an end that is also a beginning: the end of man's isolation and independence and the beginning of the Golden Age. The conclusion is also an ending that is a beginning: the end of the human race and the birth of a nonhuman entity. This parallel provides a neat and satisfying, but almost subliminal, bracket for the narrative.

These opening-ending correspondences are not the only subliminal effects in *Childhood's End.* Clarke uses both action and character to underscore his story line. The Overlords arrive and, over a period of time, establish peace and a global society. In the narrative, there is an episode by episode decline in the potential for violence. *Childhood's End* opens with cold war enemies vying to put the first nuclear rocket into space.

Hot war lurks in the wings. In the next episode, the Overlords have eliminated both hot and cold wars. All Stormgren
has to worry about is civil defiance and disobedience. In the
final episodes, there is little even to be defiant about. George
defends himself against encroaching mediocrity by retiring to
a colony dedicated to building its own artistic traditions.
Jan "creates a precedent." He challenges the Overlords' "quar-
antine" of earth. He runs away.

Clarke uses these same characters to illustrate the debili-
tating effect of a Utopia such as his Golden Age.

> When the Overlords had abolished war and hunger and dis-
> ease, they had also abolished adventure. . . . There were plenty
> of technologists, but few original workers extending the fron-
> tiers of knowledge. . . . The decline had barely started, yet the
> first symptoms of decay were not hard to discover.

The incipient loss of drive and substance is graphically
shown by an increasing blandness in Clarke's characters.
Stormgren is a strong character with many facets. Not only is
he Secretary-General of the United Nations and a renowned
poker player, he is also a student of linguistics. He works for
world peace, but there is nothing head-in-clouds about him.
He has humor, daring, self-control, and probity.

Compared to Stormgren, George lacks character. Frustration makes him sullen. He flies off the handle at criticism.
He lectures his wife on her artistic ignorance if she happens
to disagree with him. Still, George is not without strengths.
He accepts the challenge of a new way of life. He has the
courage to face his own fears. He cares about his art. For all
his weaknesses and though less of a man than Stormgren,
George is nonetheless a man.

Jan is not mature. Until the sobering experience of trying
to live on the Overlords' planet, he is scarcely more than a
boy. He is cursed with a streak of romanticism, lacks self-
awareness and objectives. He dabbles at life. He dares to
stow away on the Overlords' ship because for him there is
nothing else worth doing.

When Jan does finally mature, it is a forced growth and he remains without depth. Perhaps this is proper and logical. Could a highly sensitive individual long endure being the last man, as Jan does?

Stormgren, George, Jan: a series regressing toward immaturity and irresponsibility. If seven-year-old Jeff and infant Poppet, the first children to become nonhuman, are added to that list, the regression is almost complete. Only the womb is lacking. Perhaps Clarke is suggesting that Utopia is a sociological uterus: that such an environment is suitable only for nurturing immaturity.

The devices that Clarke uses have still another important function. The linkage between the beginning and the conclusion of *Childhood's End*, the episode-by-episode decline in the potential for violence, the character-by-character increase in blandness and irresponsibility interweave with plot and story to draw *Childhood's End* together and create a whole.

Such devices are not the only subtleties used by Clarke. *Childhood's End* is replete with suggestion and symbolism.

Dusk is falling on Taratua when the book opens, and the book is about the dusk and final night of the human race. Reinhold looks at the rocket he has built: "The ship's prow was catching the last rays of the descending sun. This was one of the last nights it would ever know: soon it would be floating in the eternal sunshine of space." Reinhold doesn't know that mankind is not destined to reach space in rockets. Yet his vision is not wholly wrong. The future he sees does not happen to man. It happens to mankind's alien offspring.

Symbolism and irony mix in the blindness of the radical leader who has Stormgren kidnapped. The physical blindness of this man is symbolic of his blindness to the good the Overlords have brought to the human race. There is also irony in his blindness. The Overlords have firmly established justice on earth. Traditionally, Justice is portrayed as blind. Clarke makes the man who rejects the givers of justice blind.

Clarke seems to delight in insinuating clues into his narrative that he knows the first-time reader will not grasp. When Karellen's ship leaves to rescue Stormgren from his kidnappers, Stormgren's assistant watches and likens the passing starships to "demon-driven clouds." This occurs long before the Overlords have shown themselves to man. Little does Stormgren's assistant know that the ships are crewed by beings who are, in appearance, Beelzebub's brothers.

Chapter 10 opens: "The human race continued to bask in the long cloudless summer afternoon of peace and prosperity. Would winter ever come again? It was unthinkable." Again, Clarke mixes symbols of truth with misdirection. The long summer afternoon will pass into night, an eternal night for the human race but, for the race, *winter* will never come again.

A final example: "For a lifetime, mankind had achieved as much happiness as any race can ever know. It had been the Golden Age. But gold was also the color of sunset, of autumn. . . ."

Such touches, and there are many more, add greatly to the texture of *Childhood's End* and to the pleasure of reading and rereading this novel.

As the exerpts quoted above suggest, another source of pleasure in *Childhood's End* is the way Clarke strings words together. His writing style is clear and easy to read. He tells his story simply and well.

Childhood's End is not all narrative, however. Vivid descriptions of real and unreal events stud the text. Consider:

High above, a meteor thrust its shining spear through the dome of the sky.

Or consider:

It was the wail of a siren, rising and falling, spreading its message of danger in concentric circles out to sea.

Or:

He clasped his arms about her waist, and the love he had once known came back to him, faint yet clear, like an echo from a distant range of hills.

Jeff's travels across the universe take the reader to some strange places. He sees "a great red sun that was beating like a heart" and later, "such a sun as no opium eater could have imagined in his wildest dreams. Too hot to be white, it was a searing ghost at the frontiers of the ultraviolet. . . ." On still another night, Jeff sees a planet outside the galaxy.

> Six colored suns shared its sky, so that there came only a change of light, never darkness. Through the clash and tug of conflicting gravitational fields, the planet traveled along the loops and curves of its inconceivably complex orbit, never retracing the same path.

Such images are difficult to forget.

Despite its somber theme, *Childhood's End* is sparked with wry humor. The huge and stately Overlords protect their eyes with dark glasses. Too large for chairs, Rashaverak the Overlord sits tailor fashion on a library floor, his tail neatly curled under him, a book in each hand and reading both books at once. Stormgren the prisoner plays poker with his jailers and leaves a bank draft to pay his debts when he is rescued.

Clarke's humor also erupts in word play. An Overlord is watching the Ouija board experiment. The owner of the board remarks: "I'd like to carry out the experiment in these rather —ah—peculiar circumstances." Clarke continues: "The Peculiar Circumstance sat watching them silently. . . ." An Overlord works "while his human hosts indulged in the frailty of sleep." George dislikes having his wife sit at his feet and lean against his legs. This was "not worth creating a fuss about. He merely made his knees as knobbly as possible." At seven years of age, Jeff "was intelligent—when he bothered to be—but was in no danger of becoming a genius." *Childhood's End* is filled with such small pleasures. Together, these evidences of Clarke's wit endow the novel with gentle charm.

Childhood's End offers the reader much: charm, humor, memorable images, sympathetic characters, suspenseful narrative, provocative themes, a simple but majestic plot. Still, these attributes do not seem adequate to account for the durability of this novel. Clarke has written a number of novels.

Most of these display similar qualities, yet none of his other books has gained as wide an audience over as many years.

Perhaps the underlying reason for the continuing appeal of *Childhood's End* is that, at core, it is myth. The attraction of myth is very great, and both the major themes in *Childhood's End* embody modern myths. The theme of the power of reason embodies the myth of the lawfulness of the universe and the accessibility of all things to reason. This is a basic myth of the age of science, and a tenet of faith in a belief system that preaches that man's rational, conscious mind can, at least in theory, comprehend all that is.

A post-Darwinian myth is elaborated in Clarke's second major theme, the power of paraphysics. This myth concerns the evolution or transformation of the human race into a superhuman or nonhuman race. Clarke has used the latter version.

Had Clarke's nonhuman entity been endowed with transcendent intelligence, there would have been no conflict between his two major themes. But he chose to give his entity psychic powers, and psychic powers violate the dogmas of reason. By choosing to give his entity such powers, Clarke created a basic and logically irreconcilable thematic conflict: the power of reason vs. the power of unreason.

To have a book end with such a central conflict unresolved could be disappointing and disturbing to the reader. This is not the case with *Childhood's End,* for myths speak to levels below the conscious mind where logical niceties do not pertain, and *Childhood's End* is myth. Moreover, despite the conflict between them, the two core myths in *Childhood's End* have the same message: Somehow, in some form, man's lineage will cope—and survive.

The universe is queer and cold. *Childhood's End* is comforting. We need our myths to keep us warm.

George A. von Glahn

A WORLD OF DIFFERENCE
Samuel Delany's
The Einstein Intersection

Samuel Delany habitually, perhaps compulsively, thinks and worries about change, about the meaning of difference—in a word, about mutability. His imaginative speculations stem essentially from a mind at home with abstraction, concerned with the causes as well as the effects of change. But that by itself should hardly surprise anyone. Talented narrative artists who have decided to write in future modes, from Wells to Asimov, usually dwell on such concerns. Mutability was Delany's central theme from the beginning. Yet *The Einstein Intersection* is something different in its treatment from anything Delany had done before. In *The Fall of the Towers* trilogy, and even more in the poetically sensitive, Nebula Award-winning *The Ballad of Beta-2*, critics recognized his versatile ideas as those of an extremely talented and intelligent writer, yet one still "young," still more clever than original in the best sense, still leaning on conventions and crafting stories of mutability as a detached consciousness. With the publication of *The Einstein Intersection* in 1967, Delany joined the New Wave of science fiction writers by choosing to deal with his concerns from the inside out. He dared the kind of self-consciousness and complexity that marks a crucial difference between the interesting hack and the artist. By becoming his own subject, he not only provoked new thought about the significance of change, he produced a declaration of artistic independence, not just for himself but for science fiction as well.

He insisted on pushing against and crossing the normal structural boundaries of science fiction. He did remain true, though marginally, to the familiar tradition of the intergalactic setting in a future time-scope of eons. Yet in the same relatively spare volume, Delany used this framework to focus on his own artistic identity crisis. He did it through an insightful use of mythology and an ironic, alter-ego character named Lobey. The sometimes intricate interplay between the cosmic and the intensely subjective allowed Delany to generate not only an extrapolation of future development. It also let him make an essentially theological statement about life's mutability, namely the possibility of an open future, at least for individuals, against the power and temptation of death in the forms of illusion and stagnation. Mutability and change suggest not only projected developments, but also, in the midst of change, the basic human need to "be," as the name "Lobey" itself expresses.

Given these elements, it would be easy enough to point to the mythology as the crucial element that binds the personal and the universal. But Delany did not set out to write a new myth; he made myth his subject. His new boldness and artistic ambition, within what had largely become a severely self-limiting genre, reflect most clearly not so much in the use of myth itself as in the choice of the character Lobey as first-person narrator of the story.

A more unlikely science fiction hero than Lobey would be hard to find. He fits none of our conventional expectations. He is not a scientist, not a prince, not a starship captain. He is a sort of nobody and doesn't even seem particularly bright. His only apparent skill is playing music on a strange twenty-holed flute-like instrument that doubles as a machete. He looks rather strange too, as in various ways do most of the story's other characters. His self-description reveals as much by tone as by fact. He is, he says, "ugly and grinning most of the time." Then he continues:

That's a whole lot of big nose and gray eyes and wide mouth
crammed on a small brown face proper for a fox. That, all
scratched around with spun brass for hair. I hack most of it
off every two months or so with my machete. Grows back fast.
Which is odd, because I'm twenty-three [Delany's age at the
time of writing] and no beard yet. I have a figure like a bowl-
ing pin, thighs, calves, and feet of a man (gorilla?) twice my
size (which is about five-nine) and hips to match. There was
a rash of hermaphrodites the year I was born, which doctors
thought I might be.

Lobey obviously, from the outside at least, is "different." He
knows it and is concerned about it.

How different Lobey is, and why, depends, of course, on the
others in his environment and on what this environment is all
about. We find in fact that Lobey is hardly alone in his concern with appearances. We are very soon somewhat mystified
by a whole group of characters immediately around Lobey,
and eventually by a whole civilization of beings whose main
preoccupation—if not obsession—seems to be genetic difference and normality. And no wonder. Physical features seem
to have run riot. The first chapter, set in a rather remote
village area of Lobey's world, contains a collection of odd-look-
ing though recognizably humanoid characters who give themselves titles of "purity" and sexually differentiate themselves
at the same time by using the prefixes Lo, La, and Le for male,
female, and mixed. Lobey is "Lo" Lobey to his fellow villagers. We meet Lo Little Jon who at twenty-four looks like "a
small black fourteen-year-old with skin smooth as volcanic
glass" and silver mesh for hair. He is contrasted with Lo Easy
who "is large (about eight feet tall), furry (umber hair curls
all down the small of his back, makes ringlets on his belly)"
and weighs some three hundred and twenty-six pounds. We
also meet briefly La Carol who is at least near "normal" looking
plus a few other seeming normals such as the wise counselor
La Dire and the practical teacher Lo Hawk. Everyone considered
at least "functional" is given one of the purity-sexual titles.
But most seem to be more or less borderline cases, like Friza,

or La Friza, who looks fairly normal, but who is suspect because she never speaks and also appears to have powers of telekinesis. Like Lobey, who apart from playing his machete-flute and occasionally herding sheep has limited social usefulness, La Friza is functional enough to be given a title. But there are also those who are completely nonfunctional, a group of genetic disasters kept in an enclosure called a "kage." Somehow, the number of total norms out of this motley mix is going down, but so are the total disasters. The majority seem to be "almosts." That explains why the La and Lo titles of purity are, at the time the story opens, being given out more laxly than in the past "to any functional who happens to have the misfortune to be born in these confusing times."

Clearly, this mix of mutants introduces the basic problem. Where is the control over the definition of normality, and even functionality, in a world so genetically unstable that its products amount almost to a circus sideshow? The chapter epigraph from Joyce's *Finnegans Wake* is beautifully apt: "It darkles, (tinct, tint) all this our funanimal world." Our world of outward "phenomena" is a jumble of "tints" and "tincts," and who can say what color is normal?

This is not a new theme for Delany. Readers of *The Ballad of Beta-2* will recall that a similar genetically-based problem of defining "total normality" reached disastrous proportions, politically, on the starships. The same terms of conflict are present here and are summed up nicely in the contrasting positions of the conservative Lo Hawk and the liberal La Dire: " 'We must preserve something,' " says Lo Hawk, and " 'Everything must change,' " says La Dire. Through Lobey's almost childlike consciousness, this perennial human debate is highlighted, focused, and personalized as he struggles to clarify his highly ambiguous place in the genetic randomness of his setting.

But genetic confusion is not the whole picture of the situation by any means. Exactly what are these characters *trying* to use as a standard of normality? The real crux, not at first noticed because Delany chooses to reveal it only gradually, is that these beings with their mixed forms and functions are not human beings at all. They are in fact from another kind of space and time, not just from another, somewhat different, world in the same region of the galaxy. They are something like psychic manifestations, although Delany is not interested in a precise explanation of what they are as such. The important point is that many years before Lobey's birth, these beings had come to settle on the long-since-abandoned Earth, and through the use of information stored in the memory-banks of huge underground computer systems have been trying, semiparasitically, to *become* human beings. Even giving birth and the whole genetic process itself seems to have been borrowed. Thus the issue of the story moves from genetics to another depth. Instead of merely the age-old question of preservation versus change, Delany explores the nature of the human. He sets alien beings in a new but previously human home that for some reason they seem not quite equipped to take over. They have tried to assume the "forms," including the psychic/mythic forms, of the past human world, but they are unable to fully realize what it means to be human. The times for them are indeed confusing.

Of course, some elements of all this are familiar enough to readers of science fiction: alien beings taking over human forms, a technological advancement evidenced by a massive computerized network in underground mazes, hints of forces still available that allow interstellar travel for these beings. All have been used by other writers. But Delany keeps their presence unobtrusive as he concentrates on Lobey and the strange physical yet psychic/mythic journey he is to make from his village to the city called Branning-at-sea. The vital questions this journey focuses—What does it mean to be human? What does that have to do with being creatively "different"? What could destroy both?—determine both the viability of these beings and Delany's own future as a writer.

That's why Delany concerns himself so much with myth in this novel. He knows that if he wants to define the human in order to affirm his own creative place within it, his central subject must in some way concern myth. He must be conscious of his own psychic involvement in Lobey's archetypical journey from the pastoral outlands to the city and the sea. Delany not only realizes this, but in passages from his notebooks occasionally used as epigraphs for key chapters, he tells the reader what he is doing as he is doing it. To give one example:

> Back outside this morning I wonder what effect Greece will have on *TEI*. The central subject of the book is myth. This music is so appropriate for the world I float on. I was aware how well it fitted the capsulated life of New York. Its torn harmonies are even more congruent with the rest of the world. How can I take Lobey into the center of this bright chaos propelling these sounds?

Mythically, Lobey obviously represents the figure of Orpheus, combined to some extent with Pan and Theseus. But to the extent that he reenacts the singer-poet-artist in confrontation with forces that would destroy his identity, he is a very modern existentialist figure with very modern choices to make. All myths have an underlying structure of meaning that remains essentially the same through myriad transformations. They are an expression of human experience. If Lobey is to be one—and perhaps the only one—from among these alien beings who achieves some contact with the truly human, he must do it by living through experiences that give a human form to his character and that allow him at the same time to transcend that form and be himself. Such a conception of the role that mythical form assumes in human identity is well expressed by Ernst Cassirer in his *Language and Myth:*

> The mythical form of conception is not something super-added to certain definite *elements* of empirical existence; instead, the primary "experience" itself is steeped in the imagery of myth and saturated with its atmosphere. Man lives with *objects* only in so far as he lives with these *forms*; he reveals reality to himself, and himself to reality, in that he lets himself and the environment enter into this plastic medium, in which the two do not merely make contact, but fuse with each other.

Lobey's "fusion" with human experience begins when death enters his life and he begins his antagonistic relationship with it. He falls in love with the telekinetic girl Friza, and she is suddenly killed. La Dire (as her name suggests, the village talker, the instructor) tells him that his mission is to leave the village and destroy whatever, or whoever, killed Friza. Thus begins yet a new version, on a future Earth, of the quest-journey of Orpheus to bring back Euridice from captive death. As Lobey talks further about himself and begins to assimilate his own information, more of the shape and condition of this world Lobey inhabits is gradually revealed, and he prepares to leave. Lobey learns that not just Friza but a number of other characters have mysteriously been taken by death and that all of these have shown certain individualizing traits that are simply described as being "different." La Dire tells Lobey that he has to travel because he too is "different." But Lobey comes only gradually to any clear understanding of the nature of this journey, learning what he needs to know through certain initiation experiences before he actually sets out toward Branning-at-sea.

Twice before his journey begins, he enters the "source cave" —one entrance, near his village, into the underground computer network. In both scenes, Delany skillfully combines the mythic and the technological. In the first descent, Lobey kills a great bull with humanlike hands, a symbolic semblance of the Bull of Minos in Greek mythology, and speaks with the computer called PHAEDRA (*P*sychic *H*armony *E*ntanglements and *D*eranged *R*esponse *A*ssociation department), in mythology the daughter of Minos. After Lobey, in the Theseus re-enactment, slays the bull, the computer tells him,

"I can remember back when there were humans. They made me. Then they all went away, leaving us alone down here. And now you've come to take their place. It must be rather difficult, walking through their hills, their jungles, battling the mutated shadows of their flora and fauna, haunted by their million year old fantasies."

PHAEDRA then tells Lobey that while they are basically not equipped for it, she supposes "you have to exhaust the old mazes before you can move into the new ones." But she also tells Lobey that he is in the wrong maze. Both the bull and PHAEDRA are in their own ways symbols of and instruments of death, but Lobey cannot know that yet. On his second descent into the cave, he meets the figure "Kid Death" on a color TV screen and learns enough about the relationship of death to this mysterious quality of "difference" to be able to formulate some clearer idea of what he is doing.

More specifically, Lobey learns, or at least comes to suspect, that death may not be all powerful. After the "different" kage-keeper Le Dorik died and yet had walked with Lobey for a while, almost in a parody of the Biblical resurrection appearances of Christ, Lobey begins to recognize some kind of reality beyond dying and can say, "If I could find what killed those of us who were different, but whose difference give us a reality beyond dying—", but that is as far as Lobey can get. After meeting Kid Death, Lobey knows enough to begin to complete that "if" clause with something like "then perhaps its defeat would give us all a reality beyond dying." But he does not know enough at the beginning of the journey to say that and to grasp what it might mean for this seemingly impossible project of taking on the "human" world. He knows only that death itself is somehow what his quest is all about and that death might be defeated.

Lobey is Delany himself, no question about that, and like Lobey, Delany was afraid when he wrote this book, apprehensive and pessimistic about his own future and about the future of civilization. What thinking person was not in 1965, and who is not now? The difference is that Delany knew the fear to be of something both inward and outward—not technology as such, not a superior destructive intelligence, not an unforeseen natural disaster—but nothing less than death itself as an essentially subliminal, interior force existing for the individual, and by extension, within the complex relationships formed by individuals. This Death is what haunted the Greeks and is what their ancient myths are basically all about. Minos represented the power of evil and death in the pre-Greek world that was saturated with images of death, from the pyramids of Egypt to the ziggurats of Babylon. The Greek victory of human life over death was expressed in the victory of the hero Theseus over the Bull of Minos in the Labyrinth and in many other mythical narratives of the life-giving power of human rationality. For us, however, that rationality has not proved to have been a victory over death but rather a new and more deadly instrument of it. Death is still what lies between man and his full realization of humanity. What confronted the Greeks and ultimately defeated them is what confronts our own more Roman-like culture. Delany sees us failing also. But by retelling the struggle against death through the attempt of another group of beings to take on the human challenge, truer terms of success might be revealed in time to save us. Or, if it cannot ultimately work for civilization, Delany the artist, in the person Theseus-Orpheus-Lobey, will show himself the way to life. Delany is afraid because he is uncertain if he, or his culture, will grow or die. And if he doesn't quite provide certainty in *The Einstein Intersection*, he does do a fascinating and often brilliant job of reminding us of the underlying psychic terms of the contest.

All this Delany explicitly acknowledges in the entry from his journal written on the Greek island of Mykonos in December, 1965, and placed at the head of a later chapter in which the journey has finally reached the city Branning-at-sea:

I remember a year and a half ago when I finished *The Fall of the Towers*, saying to myself, you are twenty-one years old, going on twenty-two: you are too old to get by as a child prodigy: your accomplishments are more important than the age at which they were done; still, the images of youth plague me, Chatterton, Greenburg, Radiguet [all of whom died young geniuses]. By the end of *TEI* I hope to have excised them. Billy the Kid is the last to go. He staggers through this abstracted novel like one of the mad children in Crete's hills. Lobey will hunt you down, Billy. Tomorrow, weather permitting, I will return to Delos to explore the ruins around the Throne of Death in the center of the island that faces the necropolis across the water on Rhenia.

On his journey Lobey uncovers as many questions as answers. What is Death really? Can it (or he) be defeated? How? at what price? These may not be questions we expect a science fiction writer to deal with, and yet Delany knows that if we are to realize who we are and where we are going, these are the questions we must come to terms with. They are in some sense the same questions Greek civilization dealt with in the myths of Orpheus and Minos. Still, in the altered outward forms appropriate to our own times, they are also ours. Technology has not excised or even modified them in any fundamental way. On the contrary, according to Ernest Becker, Norman O. Brown, and others, conflict with Death is the very generating psychic energy behind our enormous rational structures.

Like the Greeks, Delany is thus interested in Death in a far more profound sense than the cessation of physical functions in an individual body, and thus works by necessity on a plane of imagination that includes life as existing beyond physical structures. Lobey and his fellow beings are described, in fact, as having come to this world from a nonphysical plane of being. They themselves, as such, seem to have no proper "form." And the previous Earth inhabitants (the "you" to whom Lobey addresses himself as narrator) are described as having moved into another nonphysical plane, "somewhere else, to no world in his continuum." The implication is clear enough; we destroyed ourselves. Yet while that may be the result, destruction is not the real issue. There is no such thing to Delany as absolute nonbeing. He thinks of Death not as a condition of absolute nullity, but rather as nonfreedom, nongrowth. Life's real issue, as Lobey comes to discover, is whether one is to become a unique person (different) without at the same time moving completely outside group norms. Death is being under total control, having nothing uniquely individual to express or contribute to the life of the group, nothing that comes out on one's own way of looking at the world.

Another word for death in this sense is "illusion." Illusion is a controlled vision imposed from outside the self that does not allow the world and one's relation to it to be experienced "as it really is." As the basic component of death within life, it kills art. Delany knows he must conquer it or die as a creative artist. And he knows with equal intensity that his civilization is losing out to the illusion of control through technological manipulation and endless duplication. The consequences will be the eventual production of self-destructive violence. We need only think of the Nazi regime or of Dr. Strangelove.

Lobey's mythically personified antagonist, Kid Death, is a master controller of illusion and can impose it within the consciousness of other beings while he himself sits alone on a burning desert, his power unchecked by any physical constraint. We cannot fully understand the motivation or importance of Lobey's journey with Spider and his crew of dragon-herders to the great city of Branning-at-sea unless we grasp these Satanic associations of Kid Death along with his other characteristics in this many-layered mythic story. Much less will we understand the third major figure, and the last to be introduced, Green-eye, the strange companion of Lobey on the dragon-herding ride, who is explicitly identified with Christ and spoken of as the only one totally immune to Kid Death. *The Einstein Intersection* clearly has not only a pagan but a Christian level of mythic allegory as well.

Yet with all these associations present at once, Kid Death is a far more coherently and consistently realized psychological characterization than we are apt to notice on a first reading. Delany, as always, packs his pages densely. In the Kid Death scenes, as in other scenes involving beings costumed and postured, at least partially, in American popular culture images, the conventional cliches that we delight in recognizing may in fact camouflage character details that help carry the overall mythic theme. While Kid Death has his unconventionally weird aspects, like his whiteless eyes and his gills, he still comes on very much like a run-of-the-mill "bad guy" from a juvenile comic-book western; most conspicuously he wears the popularly mythologized image of Billy the Kid. But he also contains the less easily detectable traits of mythic underworld princes, Pluto, Minos, and Satan, all personifications of evil who enter into others to control and bind them.

Kid Death consistently manages to appear where he cannot be touched, always showing up suddenly in the distances or in illusionlike circumstances that reveal clearly an important aspect of his character—his deep insecurity. He first confronts Lobey, very appropriately, as an image on a color picture tube left in some part of the source cave. The killer immediately identifies himself, but only from a distance safe enough to mock the untested young avenger. Kid Death must always guard himself either by distancing or otherwise totally controlling the situation, especially potentially threatening characters. And as he says about his confinement in his desert "kage," he would close the eyes of those through whom he was looking if what was looked at frightened him. He must always be safe and in control, even when not present physically. "When what I saw frightened me, I closed the eyes seeing."

What appears to be Lobey's initial calm in the face of such a force turns out to be as much the result of ignorant ingenuousness as of courage. Lobey is still, for example, mystified by the whole process of taking over the physical as well as the soul world of the former human inhabitants. The color TV screen fascinates him and he wonders why his people don't just generate images on such screens instead of using the genetic method of reproduction "we've taken over." He is not quite able, apparently, to appreciate the importance of physical individuality for human being to be "human." Illusion and reality are not clearly differentiated, as well they might not be for a being who is essentially a psychic manifestation. This is a nice example of Delany's subtle consistency of imagination.

But this momentary fascination with the image-control capacity of TV is precisely what helps to make Lobey, as well as others, entirely vulnerable to Kid Death. So long as Lobey tends to confuse illusion and reality, Kid Death has all the power he needs to control. Yet Kid Death does not close Lobey's eyes as he has others, like Friza and Dorik, who were "different." Kid Death's own explanation for this is entirely consistent with his need to control. He tells Lobey that he is looking for *him*, not the other way around, because for some reason that Lobey is not yet prepared to learn, Kid Death needs his cooperation. Lobey has the kind of "difference" that Kid Death himself does not have and would like to control. This grotesque psychic and physical mutant called Kid Death has come out of his desert "kage" (or soon will) because he knows that something "different" has been born through the "risky" method of genetic reproduction, something beyond his ultimate controlling power. Precisely what this is, however, Delany allows us to learn only as Lobey himself gradually reaches greater self-awareness.

The next major step in that awareness involves a second, and this time physical, appearance of Kid Death. It is a more complex and revealing appearance, moreover, because not only Lobey but the Christ figure "Green-eye" become his complementary antagonists—and targets.

To begin his actual journey, Lobey joins with Spider (who is to become one of Lobey's most important teachers) and his band of dragon herders, and among them he meets Green-eye, a strange, silent figure with whom Lobey feels an instant rapport. As their drive toward the city Branning-at-Sea reaches an area Spider calls "the broken land" (a suggestion of Eliot's "Waste-land"), Lobey gets separated from the rest of the group, slips over a cliff, and while hanging by a branch is confronted again by Kid Death, this time in a bizarre parody of the serialized "western." With Kid Death is the resurrected Friza, still under total control, since whatever he kills he has the power to bring back. Sadistically, he lets Lobey hang until the very last second before he is about to slip, then shoves Friza over the side, once again killing her. On the way down, she saves Lobey's life by refusing to grab on to him in a vain attempt fails. He can control Green-eye neither by temptation nor by killing him. As Spider has said about Green-eye earlier and control. Then attention shifts to Green-eye. As Lobey scrambles up an embankment after Kid Death, he sees him at a precipice with his arm around Green-eye's shoulders. What we see this time is not a parody of a western but a version of Satan's three temptations of Christ, shortened to two. Kid Death first displays a vision of vast technological development and says, " 'I can hand you the wealth produced by the hands of them all. I can guarantee it. You know I can. All you have to do is join me.' " Then he belittles Green-eye's "difference" and demands, " 'Turn that there rock into something to eat.' " Green-eye simply ignores him and Kid Death's attempt fails. He can control Green-eye neither by temptation nor by killing him. As Spider had said about Green-eye earlier to Lobey, " 'Anyway, Green-eye just goes about his own business, occasionally saying very upsetting things to the wrong person. The fact that he's different and immune to Kid Death, from a respected family, and rather chary of ritual observances makes him quite controversial. Everybody blames the business on his parthenogenetic birth.' "

Green-eye's immunity to Kid Death seems to stem from a refusal to be attracted by illusion and from a radically non-human genetic origin. But it is not clear if Lobey's survival is more than the passive result of Kid Death's decision not to kill him. After witnessing the "temptations," however, Lobey does discover that he has some control over death himself. Lobey does "die," at least momentarily, simply by letting go his grip, and then discovers that his "difference" has resurrecting power of its own: He can bring back to life whatever he himself has killed, including himself. In the cliff-hanging and temptations episode, Lobey, in effect, resurrects himself outside the control of Kid Death. Thus both Lobey and Green-eye have, in different ways, a certain power over themselves.

Death's need to control them both and his double failure means that before they reach Branning-at-sea, Lobey, Green-eye, and Kid Death have become involved in a crucial dramatic triangle, with Lobey its apparent weak side. Later, in one of a series of interrelated explanations to Lobey, Spider

gives its meaning: Green-eye has the power of original creation, Lobey has the power of order, and Kid Death has the
power of control through illusion. "'Kid Death can control,
but he cannot create, which is why he needs Green-eye. He can
control, but he cannot order. And that is why he needs you.'"
One of Lobey's tasks is to realize what this power of "order"
in his music means for the openness of his future. He must
preserve it from death. Kid Death craves this order for himself and this lends a certain tragic pathos to his characterization. "He [Kid Death] needs patterning, relation, the knowledge that comes when six notes predict a seventh, when
three notes beat against one another and define a mode, a
melody defines a scale. Music is the pure language of temporal and cotemporal relation. He knows nothing of this, Lobey." To know order in this musical sense is to have a creative
grasp of the past so that it can be used for a new future. But
as Kid Death told Spider years before, "'The past terrifies
me. That's why I must kill it—why you must kill him for
me.'" This view of Death—as the negation of music—is consistent with his character. There is no past and no future for
Kid Death, only stagnation and illusion; he desperately wants
release, yet has nothing other than futile efforts at control
for gaining it. Afraid of both past and future, Kid Death only
distorts already created shapes into other shapes in the frantic
effort to escape an isolation he cannot comprehend.

Delany maintains his counterpointing between such psychological portraiture and historical struggle through another
explanation that Spider offers to Lobey—an explanation of
the crucial "intersection" from which the book receives its
title. While Lobey lives through the age-old mythic encounter
between growth and stagnation, a similar encounter, on a
vastly larger scale, is happening to these image-borrowing
beings. In re-creating the human past, these beings have
reached a crossing of dual strands of evolution that Spider
calls the Einsteinian and the Goedelian. Each of these needs
some separate explanation and commentary before the full
scope of Delany's purpose in *The Einstein Intersection* becomes clear.

First Spider explains a process of technological development that he associates with Einstein. This Lobey already knows about. It is easy to miss the fact that these beings among whom Lobey is trying to find his identity already possess all the advanced technology that the humans had developed. Lo Hawk and Spider, as Lobey learns, have both traveled in the galaxy at some point in their lives. All of the computers are still working. The point is that technological advancement, in the sense of manipulation of natural forces, has a limit—the limit of physical perception—and that limit had already been reached by the former human inhabitants of Earth—us —long before these beings arrived to take over the forms. That development of increased manipulative power, especially over the atom, is the "Einstein curve" as Spider explains it to Lobey. Einstein's theories had huge "visible effects" in the century or so following their formulation, but then they began to level off sharply.

Here Delany can hardly be unaware that such a "limit" set for technology has implications for science fiction itself in most of its conventional forms. After all, those Einsteinian "effects," including everything from "space-time-warps" to time-travel, have been precisely the material of science fiction during most of its history. Science fiction writers have been projecting their imaginative powers, in other words, along the convex development curve that leaped up from the inception of Einstein's ideas. Delany's acknowledgment of that developmental line and its legitimacy is what makes him a science fiction rather than a fantasy writer. But Delany recognizes that the Einstein curve has its limit, and science fiction writers, particularly in the sixties, began to approach that limit and found themselves stymied. James Blish in his *Cities in Flight,* for example, goes about as far as one can go in his conception of the super "spin-dizzies" that propel whole cities through space at faster-than-light velocity. Finally there is nothing left to happen but the self-destruction of the present cosmos and the beginning of another. How far can outer manipulative development go? What happens when all possible movements and manipulations are possible? If your thing is paving streets, what do you do when they are all paved?

But Delany, quite perceptively, posits a second developmental "curve" based on another logic altogether. This curve, starting from the same point as the other, takes a concave shape counter to it. If Einstein defined the extent of the rational, a contemporary mathematician-logician named Goedel described another way of looking at things. Goedel suggested not the outer but the inner logic of possibility. The curves may be illustrated like this:

Art to Come

Goedel's principle, as Delany paraphrases it through Spider, is this:

> "In any closed mathematical system—you may read 'the real world with its immutable laws of logic'—there are an infinite number of true theorems—you may read 'perceivable, measurable phenomena'—which, though contained in the original system, can not be deduced from it—read 'proven with ordinary or extraordinary logic.' "

In other words, look only at the system from the outside as a detached observer and a limit is reached; but look at the inner possibilities of combination within the system and no limit is ever reached. Goedel's principle, interpreted this way, is the ultimate apologia for poetry and music. It opens infinite room for art, for mythological transformations, for all conceptions of the human spirit. Only one proviso, however: The observer must become part of the dance, and thus he cannot project in advance where his steps will take him.

The Einstein Intersection may be seen from this point of view as a kind of declaration. Delany will from this point on be impatient with the limits set by the mainline science fiction assumptions. They tend to be those of the engineer, or at best the scientist, not those of the poet. The Einstein curve soon levels off on the graph to a limit; the Goedel crosses it and shoots up into infinity. When Spider asks Lobey to think about mythology in Goedelian terms, not Einsteinian, his exhortation makes quite clear the relation of Goedel's principle, as Delany interprets it, to art and its possibilities:

> "I don't want to know what's inside the myths, nor how they clang and set one another ringing, their glittering focuses, their limits and genesis. I want their shape, their texture, how they feel when you brush by them on a dark road, when you see them receding into the fog, their weight as they leap your shoulder from behind; I want to know how you take to the idea of carrying three when you already bear two. Who are you Lobey?"

Besides a body and a soul, both borrowed, how do you take to carrying a unique "I"? Lobey and his music embody the Goedelian principle: He must be "different"—his own ego—in the midst of infinite possibilities. He must distinguish order from control.

These beings have apparently had no real difficulty, except for the apparent genetic problems, retracing the Einsteinian curve from the human mold left to them, but they have no way to deal with the Goedelian, which has begun to show up in psychic-mythic forms. And Kid Death in his fear will not allow it to appear or to advance toward infinite possibility if he can help it. That is why he tries to destroy or control every being who gains some creative power, everyone who becomes "different."

The mythical conflicts in this story are not simply tacked on to the idea that these two curves at some point in human history crossed one another. Each development has its resistances to overcome and its deadly enemies; development is never merely mechanical or automatic. The physical limits of the Einsteinian are soon reached. Inner contemplation tends to slow it. The Goedelian, on the other hand, allows limitless combinations and interpenetrations, but its enemy is the stagnation of fear and the consequent need to control—inner death. To realize that the Goedelian curve or line of development (growth) exists is to realize both the existence and the infinite value of "difference." " 'The world is not the same,' " Spider says, " 'that's what I've been trying to tell you. It's different.' " It is free, that is to say, to be whatever it will be on its own terms. Simply to repeat the past is to abdicate this freedom, block the Goedelian curve, and die in distorted frustration or destruction. The risk of "being," of being "different," however, is always there too. This is the key to Lobey's name; he is Lo "Be", the acted-out principle of "being" in music, or any other ordered rather than controlled human expression. But Lobey may succeed or fail—it is not fore-ordained.

This theme also reflects an entire cultural change of focus that Delany perceived happening on a large scale, particularly among young people, during the mid-Sixties. Something was happening, and that something could be seen, or rather heard, in the music. Rock groups with some real musical art in them, like the Beatles, were described in the current slang as "something else." That is precisely how Spider describes Lobey's difference. The modern version of Orpheus was Ringo of the Beatles, the one who kept the beat.

But the human world of Ringo is gone, to wherever it went —and Lobey is in another time and place at his own inter-section between outer and inner growth. Thus the most vital choice Lobey has to make in order to become the new and "different" version of Orpheus-Ringo—an artist in his own right—is whether or not he will choose to live in the "real world," the world that is constantly changing, the one having come from someplace and the one going to someplace, but with the possibilities as infinite as music. Dove, the Jean Harlow figure of Branning-at-sea and who presides over the nightclub called *The Pearl*, whispers to him the key question directly: " 'Do you want to see what's in front of you? Or do you want to see only what you saw before?' "

What Lobey has the hardest time facing, then, is that

neither he nor the others can become just what the humans were. The implication is, besides, that the humans killed themselves because they remained trapped in myths that held no escape from Death on terms they were willing to accept. Orpheus failed; he looked back. Lobey is free to do the same. Likewise, the humans refused to take the freedom offered by Christ: a deliverance from Death and the consequent conferring of the risks and privileges of true personhood. Green-eye in *The Einstein Intersection* offers the same freedom. Lobey, however, must decide to take it. He must reject illusion and accept the ambiguous terms of the real world. Dove tells him, " 'Lobey, we're not human! We live on their planet because they destroyed it. We've tried to take their form, their memories, their myths. But they don't fit. It's illusion, Lobey. So much of it. He brought you back: Green-eye. He's the one who could have brought back, really brought back your Friza.' " But Green-eye is dead, his hanging ordered by Spider (the wise and powerful man but also the archetypal traitor). And Lobey himself delivers Green-eye's final death-blow with his flute-machete when Green-eye, hanging but not yet dead, will not simply hand him the resolution he craves: "I shrieked as outrage broke. With the hilt in both hands, I plunged the point in his thigh, sank it to the wood. I screamed again and wrenched away, quivering."

The only hope at the end of the book is that Lobey has chosen "the real" as opposed to the rest (i.e., illusion) and that since he was the one who actually killed Green-eye, he can also bring him back. "Like the Kid; I can bring back the ones I've killed myself," says Lobey. If he does so, then Green-eye (Christ) can in turn bring back Friza (love). Lobey can set this renewal in motion, however, only if his final choices have been for the real. Reflecting the ambiguity of his own mind as well as the radical uncertainty of his cultural milieu, Delany leaves the answer ambiguous.

We must not forget too that Delany's world in the mid-Sixties encompassed not just the cultural phenomena of the under-thirty intelligentsia, but also the identity struggles of the black American. This is why the theme of "difference," for all its universality, has a special poignancy for Delany. Become like the white man, the dominant culture, or become what you are? That was—and is—the form this question of freedom takes for blacks. And this is also one underlying meaning, among others, in the double nature of Lobey's flute: It can make music and it can be a weapon of power. Both uses are part of Lobey's movement toward maturity as an artist and as a free being.

The epigraph that records a portion of conversation between Delany and Gregory Corso about *The Einstein Intersection* reveals this social aspect of Delany's purpose explicitly enough: "Jean Harlow? Christ, Orpheus, Billy the Kid, those three I can understand. But what's a young spade writer like you doing all caught up with the Great White Bitch? Of course I guess it's pretty obvious." Of course it is. The lure —advertising, the transmission medium for the controlling illusions of white culture, is saturated by her sexual presence in many forms. "Dove," whose picture Lobey sees on entering the city, says in a caption, "One is *nice*? Nine or ten are so much *nicer!*" She is a version of Jean Harlow/Helen of Troy for Lobey, and it is fitting that in his Orpheus role of descending into hell to bring back Friza, he comes closest to the absolute control of death at *The Pearl* nightclub where Dove presides. The main floor is built right over a portion of the vast underground "source cave" used as the "kage" for the total deviants of Branning-at-sea. It is a pit where pure illusion presides over pure misery and degradation:

> The floor began to rotate. Through my hysteria I realized what was happening. The floor was two panes of polarized plastic, one above the other. The top one turned; the lower one was still. As they reached transparency, I saw figures moving below in the crevices of the stone, down below the chair and table legs. *The Pearl* is built over one of the corridors for the kage at Branning-at-sea. Look: they weave there among the crags, that one falling, that other, clinging to the wall, chewing his tongue and drooling blood. We have no kage-keeper here. The old computer system the humans used for Psychic Harmony Entanglements and Deranged Response Associations takes

care of their illusions. Down there is a whole hell full of grati-
fied desire—

In this striking scene, the computer PHAEDRA, her voice
thinned through the nightclub floor, gives Lobey his last warning to save himself from the fate that is overtaking his people:

> "It's still the wrong maze, baby. You can find another illusion
> down here. She'll follow you all the way to the door, but when
> you turn around to make sure she's there, you'll see through it
> all again, and you'll leave alone. Why even bother to go
> through with it? Mother is in charge of everything down here.
> Don't come playing your bloody knife around me. You've got
> to try and get her back some other way. You're a bunch of
> psychic manifestations, multi-sexed and incorporeal, and you
> —you're trying to put on the limiting mask of humanity. Turn
> again, Lobey. Seek somewhere outside the frame of the mir-
> ror—"

The right maze can only be Lobey's own. If he enters it by
choosing the real as opposed to illusion, he may also choose
to bring back the presence of Green-eye and thus ultimately
"love" symbolized by Friza. He does not have to go down to
hell to bring her back. Thus we have in *The Einstein Intersection*, besides its other layers of meaning, a mythic science
fiction Bildungsroman.

In writing it, Delany displayed at their best the chief virtues he had been developing in his earlier novels. But it
stands as a taking-off point for him, a jelling of his previous
strengths. His basic literacy and consistency of imagination
are here, along with a new and delightful note of playfulness
and lightness of touch in Lobey's characterization. The style
is richer in poetic and visionary imagery than in any of his
earlier books. Short as it is, *The Einstein Intersection* has to
be read slowly, even aloud, to be fully appreciated. And finally, Delany showed again his remarkable ability to handle
complexity of meaning in a context that never opposes realism
and fantasy. Psychic manifestations, as these beings are, cannot be classified as "fantasy," as any psychiatrist can testify.

Yet there are clearly further developments that Delany himself must have known he needed to make in his writing. His characterizations are still too undifferentiated, although he could get away with it in a story centered on myth and psychic forces. And his narrative voice is confusing at times. Why is Lobey, the narrator, telling this story in the first place? Who is he writing it for? If it is the people of the past on earth (the "you" he addresses), does he expect them to read it? How? What is the mechanism for it? The answer to that simply gets lost someplace or is ignored, along with any detailed and convincing description of just what these beings really are and where they came from. This difficulty with the framework of the narration points up, in fact, an inherent weakness in an otherwise brilliantly conceived, and for the most part, nicely wrought piece of fiction. Delany simply could not contain in this book all that he wanted to without confusing slips occurring between levels. When is Lobey Orpheus, when is he an alien "psychic manifestation" creature in semihuman disguise, and when is he Delany's alter ego? Often it all does come together admirably, but complete interpenetration of so many levels at once proves impossible.

Regina Sackmary

AN IDEAL OF THREE
The Art of Theodore Sturgeon

Theodore Sturgeon is undoubtedly one of the finest writers of science fiction today. He is also one of the most popular, for he has the unique capacity to both stimulate and entrance the imagination of his audience. Nothing makes this more obvious than the unqualified success of his script for the award-winning *Star Trek* series, entitled "Shore Leave," which had the crew of the Starship Enterprise encountering the reality of their fantasies on a planet that fulfilled every dream. That script, like many of Sturgeon's short stories, had at its center a mood and intent that has become the special feature of his work: a pervasive optimism and faith in the possibility that men and women can share in the apprehension of life as an experience that includes an abiding sense of beauty, even joy. Infused into Sturgeon's writing is the assumption that few things matter more than that people should care about one another. His stories emphasize the need to accommodate the future that may await us. And Sturgeon has the rare faculty of touching a chord of absolutes, without making of them a closed world.

The word "art" is viewed askance if it is used to refer to the literature of science fiction. Technically, there can be, perhaps, little debate. But art carries other meanings than form; it can be, ultimately, an attempt to render experience into an ideal reality—out of the imagination then comes an apprehension of mood, sensation, insight, that takes a reader beyond the ordinary understanding of things. Of all the contemporary writers of science fiction, no one makes this attempt more consistently than Sturgeon. And he takes that effort into horizons that extend our ability to perceive the inner dimension—to realize that in this fleeting existence of ours we can glimpse a utopian vision in which the act of *giving* can become a dominant impulse, a perfection of the human condition. Stories like "From Here to Easel," "Rule of Three," "Extrapolation," "A Touch of Your Hand," "Twink," "The World Well Lost," or "Thunder and Roses" have in them an implicit theme that works toward a search for unity, for wholeness—some transcendence over the impersonal reality of the modern estrangement from romantic aspiration. Above all, Sturgeon's best writing seems to project, along with a masterful storytelling ability, a desire to reinforce the idea of the community of experience—the visceral, important need for individuals to reach out and communicate what they know and understand for the benefit of everyone else. It is in this way, and by exploring the degrees of vulnerability that hold us back, that Sturgeon presents what can be viewed as a moral vision. And it is this element in its sensitivity that distinguishes his writing from that of many of his contemporaries, though the shape of his thought arises out of premises that are a distinct part of futuristic fiction.

Such fiction is a writing premised upon the suggestion that there is another way to create existence, another means of arriving at the distant point of our destiny. Even the "dystopian" literature that predicts dire consequences or envisions a doomsday record for humanity has behind it the desire to avoid what it nevertheless sees as the inevitable destruction of everything that matters. Science fiction is a genre that developed in response to the radical shift in perspective produced by the technological achievements of the nineteenth and twentieth centuries. Literature in general has always reflected or accommodated transitions in cultural attitudes and goals. Science fiction has tried to articulate the dilemma confronting the modern individual, who has to resolve a conflict between the impersonal results of scientific progress and the need to assimilate those results with his or her sense of being.

Against the indefinite and violent road along which progress leads us, Sturgeon offers a frontier of human relationships. In the *Visuddhi-Magga* of India it is written that

> This world will be destroyed;
> also the mighty ocean will dry up;
> and this broad earth will be burnt up.
> Therefore, sirs, cultivate friendliness;
> cultivate compassion.

The stars surround us; in the cold reaches of space the planets move silently through the black void. Sturgeon suggests, however, that we are not alone, that we can still question and still propose answers that will change our comprehension of purpose and each other. These are not features exclusive to science fiction; they are equally part of the mainstream of modern literature. But within the genre of science fiction they take on a special import, for it is in that literary form at its best that the basic confrontation between technological and human necessity finds its most explicit statement, and this is the most provocative theme of the twentieth century. Sturgeon proposes his response within the landscape of a triad.

A motif runs through Sturgeon's writing—his best writing —which seems to dwell upon one peculiar construction; there is an emphasis on groupings of three, an event that happens too often to be merely coincidental. The matter of dimension begins with this construction, as well as the impulse that most directly affects the tone and intent of his work. The resolution of many of his stories occurs through a fusion of the minds of three people as they come to recognize a special knowledge and sensitivity toward anything that threatens humanity. All sides have to be known, and through a deepening insight we are given by Sturgeon not something "more than human," though aliens figure prominently in his tales, but ideal humans. The tie, the link, is conveyed intuitively; there is no demonstrable character development. But through giving the *impression* of that intuition, Sturgeon creates a sense of growth and extension altogether compelling.

One story that reveals this triadic theme most directly is "Rule of Three," first published in 1951. It is a highly evocative description of the method by which an alien culture, whose members exist as "triple energy entities" attempt to destroy a virus on earth that is the real source of neurosis and isolation. The story traces briefly the lives of six people who are made aware of a new force within themselves by virtue of the influence of the unseen visitors. The tale—it is a tale, almost like a legend in its subtle workings—focuses on the limitations by which people tend to perceive one another emotionally. Sturgeon draws out of those limitations the possibility of discovering through empathy a vast and beautiful unity that transcends the private insecurities and loneliness of individuals.

The energy entities—Ril Ryl Rul and Kad Ked Kud—arrive on earth after locating the Pa'ak—"The most vicious, most contagious energy-virus known." They perceive that humanity is on the road to destruction, and decide to separate into their single parts in order to better understand the motivation of the species and to discover by what means, if any, the virus can be stopped. Each enters the mind of one human being— first Jon, a scientist, his ex-wife Edie, a girl friend Priscilla, and then Jane, a café singer, Derek, her bass player boyfriend, and Henry, a jazz pianist. Interspersed with the narrative of their separate lives are brief news reports in italics of armaments, politics, and unemployment.

A third triad emerges—Mak Myk Mok—but it is reduced to two parts when one of the human beings—the third one they entered—commits suicide. The two members are no longer complete—and in their separation they become the guardians of the first two triads, and lead all six characters toward the desired goal, which is to convince them that they too must realize their most ideal form in the triple context.

Gradually, against the background of the music of improvisational jazz, the figures move closer together. They know each other, yet do not. But along with the modulations of the music a contact begins that surrounds and envelops them in a sense of community and unselfishness. Manipulated as the humans are by the alien culture, the narrative is moving and filled with a kind of radiance. As the six meet in the café, the jazz music of Henry and Derek reflects the emotional conjoining of the two groups that had finally been effected:

> It was a modal, moody, rhythmic invention, built around a circle of chords in the bass which beat, and beat, and beat on a single sonorous tone. The treble progressed evenly, regularly, tripped up on itself and ran giggling around and through the steady structure of the bass modulations, then sobered and marched again, but always full of suppressed mirth . . . And out of the music, out of the bodies that fell into synchronization with the masterful pulse of the great viol, came a union, a blending of forces from each of six people. Each of the six had a part that was different from all of the others, but the shape of them all was a major chord, infinitely complete and completely satisfying.

The aliens have done what they came to do. The humans can assimilate the greater force of empathy, the only emotion that can make for a hopeful future. But can these six, now two triads on earth, live on without the aliens? Can they conceive the possibility of reaching not toward inevitable destruction, or conquest, but toward truth? The aliens take the six on trust, and depart to try what they can with others. For Jon, for Edie, Priscilla, Jane, Derek, Henry—the departure produces only an increased awareness of the dimension into which they have been plunged. The conclusion brings them to a new plane of existence, "as if a curtain had been lifted from their minds for the first time in their lives. . . . . something infinitely more complete. 'Cured' was the word that came to Jonathan. He knew instinctively that what he now felt was a new norm, and that it was humanity's birthright." And out of the empathy of love, the six turn their energies toward bringing their new-found understanding to the rest of the world.

The theme of the story is that of awakening. The human

beings who are the objects of an alien experiment experience revolution, a mutation, of psychic realizations. Sturgeon uses two lines in the tale from the song that controls his short story "Thunder and Roses," and they seem to hold the essence of "Rule of Three." They are "when you gave me your heart, you gave me the world," and the words circumscribe the structural element of the triads. In giving freely, the individual can change the world. In apprehending the beauty of existence, individuals are seeking that higher plane of existence; there and there only can come a cessation of violence and unhappiness. It is a theme that Sturgeon will continue to use in many of the stories that follow, along with the triadic emphasis.

"Extrapolation" pursues this emphasis. One man, a loner named Wolf whose native abilities are so unusually developed that he can do almost anything he puts his hands and mind to, is accused of an attempt at mass murder through a collaboration with an alien starfleet. A lieutenant from Washington investigates the charges, primarily in an interview with Wolf's wife, as Earth prepares to defend itself against the oncoming invasion. Despite a long report by an associate of Wolf's who witnessed the collaboration before his own death, his wife refuses to believe it. Although Wolf has a history of extreme isolation and murderous rage, she is utterly convinced that he is innocent—but the world is not and what rapidly develops is a universal cry for revenge against the man who is showing the aliens how to attack his own people. All the evidence points to his guilt.

The woman's conviction—and some deep-set honesty that is strengthened by the intuitive nature of her trust—disturbs the lieutenant. He no longer trusts his own interpretation of the situation—yet his hesitancy exists against all common sense and training. Together with this he recognizes in the woman an emotion that leaves him with a sense of emptiness—she has in her faith something stronger than he understands or possesses, something that has within it a purity beyond what the mere idea of belief could give, for it is fused with love. The denouement occurs when her faith is vindicated, for the reality is that Wolf has sabotaged the alien invasion with a cataclysmic destruction of their fleet. The lieutenant in turn, knowing Wolf's innocence will not be believed by the mob whom he has nevertheless saved, protects him and returns him to his wife. In the process, Wolf acknowledges that he has perceived that the lieutenant loves his wife and yet is yielding her to the man he once hated.

Throughout the story the impression is one of tentativeness, in which the lieutenant slowly opens up to the encompassing knowledge love can bring, and becomes sensitive to the power that shared trust can provide. He is awakened to the recognition that nothing is absolute, no circumstance gives the whole story—and that it is only through faith in another that he sees himself, and everyone, for the first time.

What Sturgeon is exploring in stories like these is the tenuous nature of communication, and the hazards we engage when we turn away from the positive forces that lie deep within us. Above all, Sturgeon is making a comment about the inevitable consequences that await civilization if it chooses to continue on the present path of alienation from any goal that does not include power struggles or aggression. The only true source of energy, the only true basis for a viable future, writes Sturgeon, lies in the willingness of individuals to put themselves aside to the degree that this allows them to accept others.

In this respect, of course, Sturgeon is directly touching on themes that have long engaged the ideas of writers who have utilized the genre of science fiction. David Lindsay in his *Voyage to Arcturus*, Arthur C. Clarke in *Rama* or Ray Bradbury in *Fahrenheit* 451 have dealt with the need to guard against the tendency to regard what is unknown as negative, to declare self-interest as primary. H. G. Wells, Olaf Stapledon, C. S. Lewis, and George Orwell—and Aldous Huxley— envisioned various forms of Armageddon that would arise out of the failure to foresee the consequences of dehumanization that they felt were a direct implication of the scientific mindset. While none of these writers rejected the advancement of scientific knowledge, they perceived that technological progress demanded an inherent distrust of the vulnerability in human endeavors. As Alvin Toffler has stated in *Future Shock,* the problem with science is not that it exists, but that its information is imposed upon a population that has not in any way been able to assimilate or accommodate the vast implications of its discoveries. Some link has to be provided, some element of a holding pattern, that puts the psychological stress at a minimum until accommodation can be made. The method is hardly an assured one; the momentum is unlikely to be stopped. But if it is not, there is no way out of the growing desperation.

Two stories by Sturgeon—"Twink" and "The Touch of Your Hand"—have a slightly different approach to the structural use of three characters.

In "The Touch of Your Hand," a girl Jubilith, who is like "the firebird's wing . . . a green meteor" in her buoyancy and laughter, falls in love with a brutal man, Osser, who is the outcast of a quiet village community. In his search for some form of power to compensate for his loneliness, he tries to build a tower that will overcome the whole population, that will subdue them and leave him victorious, a giant among men. He is an outcast because he is the subject of an experiment by the villagers. He is the only one who does not possess the shared knowledge of all things that is a composite feature of the village. As a child they had removed his telepathic sense and left him with only ordinary human perception. While they were filled with peace and the security of having access to whatever existed to be learned and understood, he remained outside that knowledge. Their motive was to understand alien "earth" cultures who had visited them, to see what, if anything, they had to be on guard against in the association with such beings. Osser was their way to understand. In the conclusion of the story, he finds that he is powerless against the villagers, who are able to prevent the invasion of another culture by methods Osser didn't even realize they possessed.

The triad here is composed of Jubilith, Osser, and Wrenn, a kind of wise man of the village, who finally helps Jubilith see that Osser is incapable of ever seeing beyond himself. He will never join the community that gives her so much serenity. To appease the stricken Osser, who dimly perceives what has happened, Wrenn hypnotizes him, returns him to his childhood to the point when the telepathic organ was removed, and leaves him there forever—happy, with a child's innocence in a man's body. And Jubilith accepts the idea of a love that must wait, and become other than passion—a love whose fulfillment comes through caring for the broken man.

In "Twink," Sturgeon supplies a rather remarkable story whose real import is impossible to ascertain until the end. The three people in this case are a father, mother, and child. The father has been in a car accident in which the mother and child have both been severely injured. As he narrates the events it is clear that he is undergoing a crisis that nearly immobilizes him. His extreme closeness to his daughter allows him to communicate with her in a telepathic way, although as a result of the accident she is deaf, dumb, and physically deformed. His wife Doris has ambivalent feelings about the bond between him and their daughter that do not have meaning until the end. A doctor named Champlain enters the picture, and convinces the narrator that he has to rally for the sake of his child—that only if he can overcome the selfishness of his guilt will he be able to help her through a necessary operation. The story then unfolds with the doctor, rather than Doris, figuring as the completion of the triad.

The unusual aspect arrives after the operation. The father-narrator has silently talked to Twink, and held the life of the child through an empathic communication in which he sensed every moment of pain and fear she endured within the silence that enclosed her. And as he leaves the operating room, and speaks to his wife, we learn that Twink has just been born, a normal child, carried through the birth trauma by the love her father extended out to her, and with the help of the doctor her injuries from the accident are reversed.

Again, Sturgeon has presented a story in which the central dilemma is the unconscious expression of incomplete emotions brought to a wholeness, a union of warmth and compassion that is a healing. As in "The Touch of Your Hand," the bond is derived from the cultivation of a telepathic communication that overcomes the normal barriers of human isolation and inadequacy. The message seems to be that one route toward a positive future lies in the development of psychic powers that may now be latent in the consciousness of humanity.

Sturgeon began writing in the early nineteen-forties, in *Astounding* magazine. After the publication of his first novel, *The Dreaming Jewels,* in 1950, he began publishing his short stories in *The Magazine of Fantasy and Science Fiction* and in *Galaxy* in the early Fifties, at which time there was a tremendous upsurge of short stories on the mass market. Some of the early works are less complex than the stories described above; they tend to represent the more adventurous or conventional forms of pulp science fiction. But one book stands out as a forerunner of the constant emphasis in Sturgeon's work on the combination of personalities working toward a unity of intuitive community—*More Than Human.*

This novel concerns six people who are transformed into a *homo gestalt,* in which their human frailties are eliminated and their natural aptitudes reinforced until what is created is a superman. The six are social outcasts who gradually join together through, again, a telepathic empathy. The story is a common feature of science fiction writing in its suggestion that such a compound personality is the last stage in the evolution of *homo sapiens.* The superhuman union that is completed is an entity greater than the sum of its parts. The theme that controls the novel is in the search for a code of morals by which the superman can become something more than a monster. As one of the six parts of the whole speaks to another—Gerry:

> "So nobody wants you and you are a monster.
> Nobody wanted me when I was a monster.
> But Gerry, there is another kind of code for you. It is a code which requires belief rather than obedience. It is called ethos. The ethos will give you a code for survival too. But it is a greater survival than your own, or my species, or yours. What it is really is a reverence for your own sources, and your posterity. . . .

Help humanity, Gerry, for it is your mother and your father now; you never had them before. And humanity will help you because it will produce more like you, and then you will no longer be alone. Help them as they grow; help them to help humanity and gain still more of your own kind. For you are immortal, Gerry. You are immortal now.

And when there are enough of your kind, your ethics will be their morals. And when their morals no longer suit their species, you or another ethical being will create new ones that vault still further up the main stream, reverencing you, reverencing those who bore you and the ones who bore them, back and back to the first wild creature who was different because his heart leapt when he saw a star."

Once again, or from the beginning, Sturgeon sees beyond the present into a vision that partakes of all that makes us what we are, what we have become, what we may conceivably be. He suggests that perfection resides in the blending of all those faculties that make us essentially human and raising them to a new height. It is an extension not into alien worlds, but into the unknown world that is part of the present—waiting to be tapped.

The appeal of science fiction is a manifold thing. On the one hand it is tied to the tradition of escapist literature, and the bizarre or erotic jacket covers of the early science fiction magazines or modern paperback editions emphasize this. Such an emphasis has a considerable role in keeping science fiction in the category of "non-literature" or at least low literature. This is unfortunate, particularly when one views the skillful writing of authors like Sturgeon. Critical evaluation has been restricted to what is termed mainstream literature—and the standards are exacting. But nothing is further from the reality of what is really happening, for in the development of modern literary expression the genre of science fiction is a vital part.

One of the reasons that the television series *Star Trek* has received such an extensive and faithful audience in the decade since its completion is because of a quality it possesses beyond the excitement of "exploring strange new worlds."

It approaches the subject of the final frontier with a visionary statement about the necessity of sustaining the rich and diverse substance of human contact and friendship. A "three" exists there, too, in Kirk, Spock, and Dr. McCoy. Perhaps Sturgeon's idea has an attraction that is more than philosophical, but which in addition speaks to a great need in the human heart for a closeness—an integrity of closeness—that is all too often denied in the modern credo.

In the concept of new horizons, we experience a correspondence to the dimension within us. Our presence is a microcosm, we perceive, of a larger scheme. If that more vast entity is nothing more than an endless void punctuated by white dwarfs, super novas, and black holes, the very infinite quality of the space precludes our believing that we know for sure. And therefore, we assume that our individual capability and potential can be plumbed, and perhaps through the inner search we will discover what exists beyond. Science fiction explores both dimensions, if it is sincere. It is when both dimensions are touched that science fiction as literature is authentic, and in this Theodore Sturgeon is most representative.

9

David N. Samuelson

STRANGER IN THE SIXTIES
Model or Mirror?

Robert A. Heinlein may be the quintessential American science fiction writer, but he was never happy being restricted to an audience that normally read only science fiction and fantasy. It is true that he established his reputation before World War II by introducing a certain amount of realistic detail and context into adventure stories of space and the future. After civilian service in the war, however, he lost no time in trying to bring his vision of that "modern" kind of science fiction to a wider audience.

During the next decade and a half, his stories were published largely outside the science fiction magazines, in the *American Legion Magazine*, *Argosy*, *Blue Book*, *Boy's Life*, *Saturday Evening Post*, *Short Stories*, and *Town and Country*. Meanwhile, he was almost inventing the "juvenile" science fiction novel, aimed at capturing an audience just entering that stage of adolescence, the continuation of which is addressed by most "adult" science fiction.

In a Heinlein juvenile, a young boy typically (one was a girl) grows to maturity, in the process of living through and effecting events projected into our next century, by means of making decisions that involve his intelligence and mold his character. Reached at a vulnerable stage of their development, there is no telling how many teenagers in the Fifties went to Heinlein to have their vision shaped of now as well as then, since our present is well into their future.

That vision was like Horatio Alger's in some ways, not only because it gave its readers a sense of their own potential, but also because it made clear that this potential could be limited as well as enhanced by scientific, technological, social, and psychological factors. Since Heinlein's juveniles are still popular in libraries, and are never out of print, millions by now must have been introduced by them to the concepts of science fiction, to science fiction as myth, and to science fiction as literature.

It was not until the Sixties, however—when Heinlein himself was in his fifties—that he became a really popular writer for "adult" audiences, known to large numbers of people outside the science fiction subculture. Perhaps it would be more accurate to observe that a greater proportion of society became initiated, if only minimally, into the science fiction subculture. The growth in Heinlein's sales and reputation was gradual, centering on one book, which shared with Frank Herbert's *Dune* (1965) the dubious blessing of becoming an "underground classic." *Stranger in a Strange Land* (1961) sold well over a million copies, improved the market for the sale and revival of his other books, and made it possible for his two long, rambling, ostensibly sexy and philosophical novels of the Seventies to become best-sellers virtually on publication. From being a rival of Isaac Asimov and Arthur C. Clarke, Heinlein came to compete with Harold Robbins and Jacqueline Susann, although his idiosyncrasies made it unlikely he would ever surpass them.

Stranger in a Strange Land did a number of other things, too, that made it in some ways emblematic of the Sixties. As a work presumed to be science fiction—though the connection was not emphasized in promotion—it suggested to the public that the genre had possibilities for objects other than adventures in outer space and cautionary tales of horrific futures. It fit the iconoclastic mood of the times, attacking human folly under several guises, especially in the person or persons of the Establishment: government, the military, organized religion. By many of its readers, too, it was taken to advocate a religion of love, and of incalculable power, which could revolutionize human affairs and bring about an apocalyptic change, presumably for the better.

The ugly side of this reading was illustrated by the strange case of Charles Manson, self-appointed Messiah of Southern California, who apparently found in this book, as in the Beatles' song, "Helter Skelter," a cornerstone of his own religion of love *and hate* that culminated in the Tate-La Bianca murders of 1969. The publicity attendant upon the Manson trial brought unwanted notoriety to an author already jealous of his privacy, individualism, and self-determination. But this was not the only sign Heinlein had that *Stranger* appealed to slightly unbalanced minds. In comments appended to manuscripts given to the library of the University of California, Santa Cruz, he commented, relative to this book, "I still think it is a good story (but nothing more)—and I must confess that I am startled at the effect it has on many people —especially when I receive letters starting 'Dear Father Jubal.' " Nor was the Manson trial likely to end the "misinterpretation" of this novel; there are cults in Southern California, and I have heard elsewhere, that use *Stranger* and some of Heinlein's other works practically as sacred texts, for their "water-sharing" and sexual rituals, and their mystical outlook on life.

The Manson publicity and the "water-brotherhood" cults may give us pause in trying to evaluate this curious book. Heinlein's fantasies may not be directly responsible for the actions of a warped mind or for other echoes of this novel in the frantic period the author once predicted would be called "the crazy years." But it may be impossible, except in the most sterile and clinical terms, to judge this book solely on intrinsic grounds, such as matters of form and style, plot and character, artistry and craftsmanship. With any "popular" work, matters extrinsic to the text are of signal importance, too. The artist and his audience are in a symbiotic relationship; they must be ready for him, and he must validate their view of the world. I do not pretend to know to what extent *Stranger in a Strange Land* was cause or effect of the social patterns it reflects, but I am certain its popularity has not been due simply to literary excellence. Its importance as a social document, as a representative artifact of a stage of Heinlein's career, and as a harbinger of the phenomenal popularity of science fiction and related art in the late Seventies, far outweigh whatever merits or demerits I claim for it as a work of "speculative fiction," a term preferred by Heinlein.

Before examining these other aspects, however, it may be well to examine just how it does function as literary art. In its simplest form, *Stranger in a Strange Land* pretends to answer the question, "What would happen if a Man from Mars were to come to Earth?" Formally, it combines some elements of the science fiction thriller with two conventions popular in the eighteenth century as vehicles for holding up society to ridicule or admiration. In the first case, a visitor from an exotic land—Persia for Montesquieu, Jupiter for Voltaire in "Micromegas"—tries to understand the customs of the writer's world; or, like Swift's Gulliver and Defoe's Crusoe, the emissary of our civilization brings his customs with him when visiting someone else.

In the second case, the *Bildungsroman* or "novel of education or development," the writer traces the personal growth and education of a young man (usually), from childhood to maturity, dropping him before he does the presumably great things for which he is destined. This pattern is familiar from Heinlein's juveniles, but here it is extended back to more primitive roots in the tragic hero, or more precisely, the dying and resurrected god whose sacrifice implies immortality for all his followers.

In other words, the Man from Mars, if he came to Earth, would see what a sham our society is, but would become educated in it to the extent that he could combine Earth and Mars realities, attempting to bring the combination to others. Since Earth is not ready for such changes, however, he would be "punished," although the punishment would be in vain, since he is immortal and so is his legacy.

Setting this frame in the near future, Heinlein draws on the resources of science fiction to help make his story plausible. Some of these conventions, dubiously anchored in

1961, are sheer fantasy in 1978, and others were sheer fantasy to begin with. Though for some readers, this mixture is self-contradictory, preventing anything in the book from being taken too seriously, for others, the uncertainty is not a factor, or functions to give the impression that anything in fact is possible, if you know how to wish for it.

How important the story is for the book may be a matter of controversy. Heinlein himself maintains that with *Stranger* he realized that his readers really wanted to hear more philosophy from him, that the story was simply a frame on which to hang his observations. Certainly that is true of *I Will Fear No Evil* (1970) and *Time Enough for Love* (1973), the two novels of the Seventies that appealed much more to the general public than to the critics. And philosophizing there is in *Stranger*, in good measure, filling out the outline not simply in the satirical perceptions of the Man from Mars, and his elder alter ego, Jubal Harshaw, but also in the development of the mingled Earth-Mars religion that the "visitor" establishes. But the meaning of all this talk is very dependent on what happens, both to the Man from Mars, and his mentor, who stand in for Christ and the "doubting" apostle, Thomas; if their opinions have any meaning at all, it must be supported by their actions and reactions in a story with heavily mythical reverberations.

Beginning "Once upon a time," the book has mythical pretensions that are visible immediately. Part One, "His Maculate Conception," has parodic designs upon the traditional hero story, with Jesus as the most obvious object of the parody. Born on Mars, Valentine Michael Smith, his name calling up associations with a saint, an archangel, and Everyman, is the "legitimate child of three parents." Progeny of an adulterous ("maculate") affair among crew members of the first manned expedition to Mars, he clearly was conceived under unusual circumstances, and after the crew members died, he was raised by the local fauna, though they are not the "animals" or "humble people" of the traditional hero myth. Rather, his "foster parents"—to whom both parts of the concept would be incomprehensible—are Heinlein's version of the legendary inhabitants of Mars, popular in science fiction since before the turn of the century, and featured in his earlier juvenile novel *Red Planet* (1949).

Unwilling, until the "Old Ones" insist on it, Smith accompanies members of Earth's second Martian expedition, twenty-five years after the first, on their return home. There he is kept in hospital seclusion, ostensibly because of his need to adapt to Earth gravity and his unfamiliarity with human language and customs, even females. Actually, he is being detained because under Earth law he is supposed to be not only heir to the fortunes of his three parents, but also the "owner of record" of the entire planet of Mars. Ben Caxton, an anti-administration news columnist, gets wind of this virtual imprisonment from his girl friend, Gillian (Jill) Boardman, a nurse at the hospital, whom he persuades to plant a bug in Smith's room. When Ben disappears mysteriously, Jill spirits Smith out of the hospital in a nurse's uniform, and takes him to Ben's apartment. There they are invaded by police, whom Smith makes disappear, before withdrawing into himself at minimal levels of respiration and circulation.

Given what follows, this adventure-story opening seems structurally inappropriate, though it does draw the reader into the action, waiting to see what happens next. If we grant that, on Earth terms, Smith is still only a child, even an infant, it also gives another meaning to the title of "Part One," in which he is "born again" on Earth.

"His Preposterous Heritage," the title of Part Two, suggests, of course, his inheritance, and his Martian upbringing, as parts of it are gradually revealed. But it also brings in associations of his cultural heritage from both Mars and Earth, with specific reference to the basic survival training for social life among the humans he receives at the hands of Jubal Harshaw and his retinue in the Pocono Mountains of eastern Pennsylvania. In by far the longest section of the book, Heinlein takes on the established order in both plot and commentary. In his cultural infancy, "Mike," as he has come to be known, comes under the tutelage of an elderly eccentric, who is a doctor, a lawyer, and a writer of commercial fiction, and who becomes in effect Mike's guardian. Rather than duplicating the "foster parents" motif, this part of the story recalls the wise advisor many mythic heroes come upon just as they are setting out on their adventures. But rather than simply preparing Mike for the world as it is, or as it should be, Jubal concentrates for the most part on what's wrong with the world.

The machinations of the plot require that Jubal, rich and wily, outfox the SS (Special Service) men of the World Federation, gain access to Secretary-General Douglas through the medium of his wife's astrologer, and engineer a three-ring circus that gets Mike off the hook as far as his alleged possessions are concerned. Jubal finesses Douglas into a *de facto* recognition of the Man from Mars as a foreign ruler, then as ambassador for the Martian Old Ones, who have some prior claim to their planet. Then he proceeds to disencumber Mike from the fears and worries of managing his economic inheritance, by making Douglas himself Mike's "attorney-in-fact," freeing Mike simply to spend whatever he needs from his income.

But money is only part of his "preposterous" heritage; the more important parts are cultural, bi-cultural to be exact. Martian-raised, Mike is at least bemused by the cultural set of Americans, as he comes to understand it by listening to Harshaw, reading the encyclopedia, watching the stereovision, etc. From his Martian standpoint, human religion, fear of death, and sexual inhibitions are absurd. But Jubal and his band also learn about Mike's Martian heritage, at least as preposterous from a human standpoint, except that Mike can show its validity. He is capable of suspended animation, astral projection, telekinesis, and of willing out of existence objects, including people, in which he "groks wrongness." Later we find that he can read minds, change his body shape, and make love in a superior manner, besides that, he's immortal.

This heritage, we are told, reflects his Martian training, which is wrapped up or encoded in the Martian language, fragments of which we are invited to learn. The importance of water to a dry planet leads to "water sharing," an intimate ritual among "water brothers," who attempt to "grow together," perhaps so that their "eggs share the same nest." Short on food, the Martians don't believe in wasting it, thus they practice ritual cannibalism, especially of the bodies of those they hold in high regard. When the body "discorporates," however, the Martian becomes an "Old One," helping to "govern" the society, if that is a meaningful term for a way of life that is unchanging over millennia. Given this stability, and the absence of death, the Martians have a very patient attitude toward the passage of time. "Waiting is" is a common Martian expression, embodied also in Mike's sense of his youth and immaturity, as indicated by his self-critical observation, "I am only an egg." Their time-scale is suggested by the millennia they have spent considering the aesthetic, rather than ethical, questions raised by their destruction of the fifth planet, where the asteroids are. We are told if they ever turn their attentions seriously toward Earth—Mike is a temporary "spy" for them, unknown to himself—they will probably destroy it, too, because of the "wrongness" that is here for them to "grok."

"Grokking" is the central term of the Martian language, according to the linguist aboard *Champion*, the returning spaceship. It signifies "to know," but in a holistic way, which includes both intellect and intuition, and physical and ethical factors as well. It is absolute, unquestioning, and instant, as a god's or an angel's knowledge perhaps should be, and as merciless and unmoved by human failings and humane considerations as a god's or angel's perhaps should not be. It is so redolent of the divine that Mike eventually translates it as a pantheistic paean, or term of address: "Thou art God."

As if this education were not eccentric enough, Part Three is entitled "His Eccentric Education." It includes his discovery of money as an idea, a symbolic structure. It includes his visit to the Tabernacle of the Fosterites, a delicious parody of contemporary commercialism in the service of Christianity, complete with slot machines and cheerleaders, which ends with Mike "discorporating" Bishop Digby because he "groks wrongness." Following immediately on that is his initiation into sex, which he comes to realize is a better "growing together" than what he knew on Mars, because it involves the body and "knowing" the whole person.

Leaving Jubal, who has a carnival past of his own, Mike takes Jill into carnival life for a time, but his "extra-sensory" powers aren't convincing enough as magic, because he doesn't have enough showmanship, enough sense of the difference between performers and "marks." But showmanship, salesmanship, art, and sex begin to come together when he and Jill see the "sacred" Fosterite illustrations on the tattooed lady, Patty Paiwonski. Jill gets an engagement as a Las Vegas showgirl, and learns to see herself through the eyes of her male customers, with the aid of Mike's telepathic abilities; from her earlier prudery, she has become practically wanton, though the change is abrupt and not clearly motivated.

What is missing, however, in Mike's makeup, is a sense of the tragic—since death and even loss are practically impossible concepts for Mike to understand—and of the comic, which are closely aligned. Mike has always been afraid of laughter: the physical act itself seems painful, though it supposedly brings joy. He finally learns to appreciate the irony of it by watching monkeys in a zoo. Beaten by another, the first monkey doesn't fight back, but rather takes out his frustration on another, smaller monkey, totally uninvolved in the original hostility. Mike laughs uproariously, recognizing both the pain and goodness in laughter, suddenly coming to understand the role of exploitation in serving both the exploiter and the exploitee. Feeling pity for humanity, which doesn't have to live that way, he believes, he is now freed to do something about it, and to use what he has learned in order to do it.

His "education" was aimless, in the sense that he was not conscious of any fixed purpose. He had just drifted, letting his unconscious mind sort things out, as he followed in the footsteps of his "father," Jubal. But what was cynicism in the old man becomes zealous idealism in the young "alien." Having found the secret of the complementarities of joy and pain, love and death, Siva and Kali, Mike now moves offstage, to be presented primarily from the viewpoints of Ben Caxton and Jubal.

Part Four is called "His Scandalous Career," a title more fitting before the rise of so many new cults in the Sixties, and the so-called "sexual liberation" of the Seventies. Since Mike has found a "utopian" vocation and utopias are notoriously hard to make interesting, Heinlein backs us away to see him at a distance. Jubal, having followed Mike's career through the Union Theological Seminary and the military—from both of which he was thrown out—through college to ordination as a preacher, is contemplating sculptures, when Ben bursts in on him. Before he will listen, Jubal must explain something about art, in a "literary" manner, looking for the story in the statue. His favorites are by Rodin, women whose characters have grown through adversity; now he is meditating on "the Little Mermaid,' caught between two worlds, and pontificating that all "creative art is intercourse."

His pupil clearly has gone beyond him, as Ben, in flashback, recounts his visit to Mike's Church of All Worlds. Art and intercourse are both involved, as is the female body, specifically those of Jill and Patty and Dawn Ardent, former Fosterite showgirl now virtually identical with Jill by dint of Mike's willing it. Mike's new cult combines the sexual growing together of humans with the psycholinguistic perceptions and powers of Martians. But Ben, who lusted after Jill in Part One, can't cope with the possibility of a threesome with Jill *and Mike*, and splits, only to have Jubal tell him his problem is jealousy. Intellectually persuaded, perhaps, that Mike's religion is a boon, but unconvincing in his rationalizations, Jubal does argue Ben into going back to the "nest" to join the perpetual sacred round.

Given the readily outraged state of public morals in America, as demonstrated by past history of utopian communes and polygamous marriages, it was logical to assume in 1961 that the Church of All Worlds would be destroyed by the general public. Indeed, Part Five, "His Happy Destiny," opens with the news that the Church has been burnt down, presumably by outraged Fosterites, though Mike and his cohort escaped, and Jubal joins them in a posh Florida hotel (which they own, since their enterprise pays, and pays well). Mike's followers are preparing a Martian dictionary to help them train an even bigger cadre of disciples, who will help to overturn a corrupt society. But there is a sense of expectation in the air, which Jubal can not help but feel is ominous.

Preparations apparently are being made for Mike's "crucifixion," though Mike himself seems to be waiting for a blessing from Jubal before he goes through with it. After their "last supper" with Mike, there more in spirit than in body, Dawn persuades Jubal to enjoy sex with her; he does—comes the Dawn—and the entire nest, he discovers the next day, shares their ecstasy. To some extent convinced, Jubal argues with Mike that he has a "fine system—for angels," but that humans are not Martians and can't bear the responsibility of being gods; he has visions of Rodin's "Caryatid Fallen Under Her Stone." If it is valid, Jubal argues, the Martian discipline is bound to win; then Mike should not simply talk about its superiority, he should show it. With this cue, Mike presents himself to the mob outside, strips off his clothes, and allows them to stone him to "discorporation." Mike's "angelic" followers are awed by his showmanship; only Jubal, the nonbeliever, seems to feel the loss, as of his own child.

Heartbroken, Jubal almost dies of a stroke, but is convinced that his life is saved by the discorporated Mike, whose bodily essence, in a broth, he shares with other nestlings (accompanied by the pun, "Mike always did need a bit of seasoning)." Finally won over, like the apostle Thomas, Jubal dictates that a statue of Mike be erected on the spot, decides it's time for him to learn Martian, and begins to write a stereoplay based on the events of Mike's life—a modern gospel, something like *Stranger in a Strange Land.* Lest all of this be taken too seriously, however, Heinlein shifts back for the final chapter to a setting in a comic heaven he has used several times since the discorporation of Bishop Digby.

Having been abandoned by the Martians at the beginning of Part Five, Mike is now revealed as the Archangel Michael, as Patty had intuited some time before. He is Digby's superior, who is now convinced there are "a lot of changes he want[s] to make," though we have it on good authority—from the angel Foster, originator of Fosterism, whom Digby himself originally discorporated—that one basic rule of heaven is that you can't affect what goes on down on Earth. In one sense, this exchange may mean that heaven is underwriting the revolution Mike started on earth, but the changes desired by the Archangel Michael are not explicit. And the comic book quality of the heaven scenes, cutting across the equally implausible, alternative presence of the Martians as manipulators, is not such as to inspire confidence in the sincerity of the conclusion.

This long summary suggests some of the complicated nature of this book, and some of the problems involved in trying to deal with it as an aesthetic object. Its choppy structure, unrealistic characters, talky presentation, frequently banal style and inconsistent tone immediately mark it unsatisfactory by most literary criteria. But the plausibility of its science fictions, the isolated effectiveness of some of its scenes, the coherence of Mike's world-view and the logic of its unifying symbols suggest that something other than realistic criteria may legitimately be invoked.

At the center of the story are Mike's martyrdom and Jubal's apostolic succession, Heinlein's ambivalence toward which is responsible for the uncertain, hybrid manner in which the tale is told. Solipsism, Heinlein's frequent subject, is in conflict here with an exemplary myth of men like gods, and both offer subjective guidance to the willing reader. Given the receptivity of his audience in the Sixties, *Stranger* had to be particularly effective. Moreover, its success seems to have redirected Heinlein's fiction in the Seventies, and may have realigned the whole science fiction spectrum, in quest of a larger mass audience.

To take up aesthetic matters first, the novel is uneven at best to a critical reading, which values the shape and style of a book, its consistency both internal and with the world outside. The five parts of this book are oddly made and oddly connected, reflecting an indeterminacy of form, caused perhaps by a changing conception of the work in progress, or a willful misleading of reader expectations. Idiosyncratic manipulation of point-of-view is perhaps the most blatant example, but it reveals an inconsistency of focus and other discontinuities of style and approach.

An omniscient narrator gives way to Jill, as fairy tale becomes first historical chronicle, then cops-and-robbers melodrama in Part One. Part Two belongs to Jubal, despite an introductory chapter concentrating on the Secretary-General, his wife and her astrologer; some glimpses at the world through Mike's eyes; and momentary recursions to the cosmic viewpoint of the Martians. Jubal's skeptical pragmatism sounds the dominant tone, but the other viewpoints are progressively farther removed from it, and Mike's demonstrations of his prowess undermine both Jubal's and the reader's incredulity. Jubal's objects of ridicule Mike takes seriously in Part Three, seen primarily through Jill or Jubal; Mike's viewpoint is adopted briefly twice, and the new cosmic viewpoint of the cosmic angels is introduced. Though omniscient observations begin it, Part Four looks at Mike entirely through Ben's reporting and Jubal's editorializing. Finally, framed by Martian and "heavenly" viewpoints, Part Five sees Jubal capitulate to an increasingly ethereal Mike.

Given this arbitrary jumping back and forth and around, a reader is unsure of what to focus on. Mike is in the background, then the foreground, then the background; Jubal is a filter, then Ben is a filter for Jubal. On the outskirts of the action, the omniscient narrator sometimes exposes us to the general follies of mankind, the millennial meditations of the Martians, and the uninspired horseplay of the supposedly comic angels. Which will it be, as critic Alexei Panshin irritably wonders, an adventure-story, a satire, or the founding of a new religion?

The adventure story all but dies midway through Part Two, and Ben Caxton, one of its major players, now delivered into Jubal's care, becomes a nonentity. The satire changes direction in Part Four, when Jubal starts taking Mike's Church seriously and criticizing Ben's opposition to it; satire is nonexistent in Part Five, except for the heavenly frame. In order for the "good story" of Mike and his Church to gain full sway, the settings and the characters become little more than props.

Although one seldom knows what Heinlein's characters look like in any of his books, where they go and what they do are usually clearly visualized. But Mars, this time around, is a shadow of its former self in *Red Planet*. Jubal's house has fourteen rooms and ample acreage, a pool and rose bushes, stereovision and sculptures, some warning devices and lots of beds, but none of it has any dimension or presence. Most solidly there are the conference room where the "treaty of Mars" is arranged, the Fosterite Tabernacle and Mike's Church, and two of them, if not all three, are caricatures.

The characters are a mixed lot, none of them substantial from a realistic standpoint. Secretary-General Douglas and his retinue, and the officers of the *Champion*, are at least stereotypes, which gives them an edge over the military and hospital personnel, the various Church members, and Jubal's staff—gardener and mechanic (male), three secretaries (female)—who are nonentities. All fulfill plot functions but little else. Douglas is a falsely folksy politician, whose shrewdness is in question when he lets Jubal maneuver him so easily. His women are mainly "media," enabling Jubal to reach Douglas; the astrologer reminds Jubal of his carnival past and the wife is killed off arbitrarily in Chapter 30 (under a change of name, surely a careless inadvertence). The *Champion's* linguist, an Oxonian Arab, interprets a little for Mike, offers a cultural contrast to two grotesque Jews in Mike's Church, and eventually weds one of Jubal's secretaries. Jubal's mechanic, Duke, is a foil: outraged by Mike's professed cannibalism, he gives Jubal an excuse to attack Kansas provincialism—Heinlein was raised in Kansas City (Missouri)—then has an unmotivated change of heart strong enough for him not only to accept Mike, but even to ply his trade in Mike's Church as a full-fledged "water brother." We are told that all of the secretaries are beautiful and intelligent, but other than take dictation from Jubal, they are used essentially as kitchen help, and later as bedmates (two of them get radiantly pregnant, probably by Mike).

Of the "major" characters, Ben and Jill are hopelessly inconsistent, if viewed as people rather than functions. A hard-nosed news columnist, Ben Caxton is dumb enough to fall into the hands of the Special Service, though he knows he is on their hate list. After trying in vain to seduce Jill in Part One, he proposes in vain in Part Two, after her efforts helped rescue him, then leaves off the chase, for no reason. Presumably having seen the seamy side of everything, he develops in Part Four a sense of prudery strong enough to wilt an adolescent's erection. Robert Plank in his essay on the book, appropriately calls it fear of homosexual encounter, but Jubal misdiagnoses it as "jealousy," and Ben takes Jubal's advice to go back and claim his piece of the action.

Jill's case is even more curious. Though we are told that men are a "hobby" with her, she doesn't respond to Ben's advances, though she's clearly attracted to him. A capable nurse, once she gets to Jubal's, she becomes virtually a fourth secretary, chiefly distinguished by an inordinate repulsion to Duke's pornography collection. She would seem ill-suited to educate Mike in "naughty" poses or to become a Las Vegas showgirl who has what the customers want, but she flips completely from prude to wanton. With no possessiveness at all, the least one would expect from someone so apparently obsessive, she shares Mike with Patty the tattooed lady, and then with anyone else in the nest. Her utter selflessness—or sheer functionality—is underlined in the Church by her total interchangeability with Dawn Ardent, the former stripper and Fosterite. She is so inconsistent, in sum, that Panshin aptly says "at any time it would not surprise me for her to unscrew her foot and stick it in her ear—she is capable of anything." Consistency is out of the question for the series of functions Heinlein has tried to unite in one convenient "character."

The only characters approaching depth or consistency are Mike and Jubal, though they take some abrupt turns, too, and are in some ways different versions of the same person, as we shall see later. Even more than the others, they are predominantly talk, especially Jubal. One of his functions, of course, is just that, to talk, to act as a mouthpiece for Heinlein's observations, some of them scathing, on the contemporary (1960) scene. Jubal pronounces judgments on art, sex, religion, politics, cultural taboos, the general state of society and commercial writing, among other things, most of them reflecting a certain amount of cynicism from an old man who has lived "most of a century" and who supposedly has seen everything. But he can't stop talking, about anything and everything, even if he contradicts himself, or violates the good sense he is also supposed to represent in contrast to the dictates of custom. Even the two actions with which he is actually credited—getting the police, and then his inheritance, off Mike's back—are the result of talk and his "big mouth" is in some sense responsible for Mike's martyrdom.

Mike, too, talks much of the time, expressing either his ignorance or his learning, and his followers do the same. Though he does take action onstage—discorporating guns, ashtrays, helicopters, people—most of his work is offstage, and we simply see him ruminate about it or preach the virtues of his Martian discipline and the wonders of Earth taken for granted by its inhabitants. Since mastery of the Martian language is supposed to be the key to his religion, as well as to his superpowers, talk is perhaps appropriate, but so much of it is essentially irrelevant to the adventure, the satire, or the religion. A lot of it is simply backchat, exchanges between Jubal and others intended to be funny; most of it is banal, both in content and style. People call each other "bub," "m'dear," "little lady," "Stinky," and "junior," and frequently intersperse an "uh" into their discourse; they talk in cliches or undigested academese, whether they've been initiated into the Church, or even translated to heaven.

Nowhere, perhaps, is Heinlein's inconsistency more irritating than in his refusal to establish a position from which the whole farrago can be viewed. Ben and Jill are clearly misguided, since Mike can more than handle any physical danger.

Jubal is obviously unequipped for the kind of commitment Mike wants from him. Mike's adventures on Earth are hardly in keeping with the comic heaven he shares with Digby and Foster. And that heaven and reality as seen by the Martians seem mutually contradictory. The deepening tone as the story goes on suggests taking Mike and his Church seriously, but the makings of his religion are preposterous—and are so labeled within the book—and his own immortality removes any tragic sting from his death.

It is as if Heinlein had been seized by a story with its own inexorable logic, then sought to undercut its effectiveness by devices that might absolve him of responsibility for the story's message. Panshin maintains Heinlein never could end a story right, because he was unwilling to accept anything more meaningful in life than search and survival. The commitment in this story was to nothing less than martyrdom, the myth of the dying god whose demise liberates his followers; but being forced into the position of offering that lesson to his readers seems to have been unacceptable to Heinlein's better judgment.

For all that it fails to work as a realistic novel, however, *Stranger* is not totally removed from the plane of the plausible, and it does have a symbolic coherence. Heinlein is a master of telling details that set up a plausible future, and that talent, though subdued, is still present. Though the difference between a "winchell" and a "lippman," as generic names for kinds of news columnists, depends on one's memory of the novel's past, other details are more future-oriented. However, it's a nostalgic future, not dense with probable twenty-first century concerns. Spaceships, aerocabs, 3-D stereovision, and automatic kitchens are familiar science fictional apparatus, as is the image of Mars as a dying planet with an old and wise civilization. Though this picture was thoroughly demolished by the Viking Landers, it still has the power to command fictional suspension of disbelief. There are also a couple of new things. The stereo features commercials for "Wise Girl Malthusian Lozenges," Ben's apartment has a carpet of living grass and Anne, one of Jubal's secretaries, is also a

"Fair Witness," bound to testify only to what she actually senses, not to inferences drawn from her impressions.

Then there are the objects of Heinlein's satire, some of which are succinctly summed up, if not by the narrator's brief notice, then by Jubal's dismissal. There are periodic "news summaries," in which the narrator fills us in on typical head-line stories of the day, far from our concern with the story itself, and geared more to 1960 than to the turn of the century. And there is the stereovision itself, the "obscene babble box," which introduces Mike to Fosterism, and later broadcasts his martyrdom, in an exercise in sheer crass commercialism not far removed from the excesses of American television today. On at least three occasions, moreover, there are excuses for full-scale "cartoons," that are effective comic scenes.

When the SS come to take the Man from Mars away from Jubal's house, Mike is obediently hiding in the murky pool, but his disembodied consciousness watches everything from above and whisks the threatening men and machines out of existence, making him a murderer without ever losing his innocence. In a sustained piece of manic invention, Jubal frantically searches for and finds a direct link to the Secretary-General, just as the door to his mansion is broken down. Jubal then gets the officer in charge a dressing down for not having the arrest warrant Jubal knows full well disappeared with the first group of lawmen.

When the Man from Mars and his retinue arrive for nego-tiations at the Executive Palace, Jubal brushes aside minor officials to take advantage of the scheduled media circus. He lets Mike be interviewed, sees him reunited with his friends from the *Champion,* then demands half the conference table for the delegation from Mars, including the spaceship crew, a Fosterite Senator, and a dignitary often forgotten at such functions, the President of the United States. In the negotia-tions that follow, Jubal, unfazed by diplomatic niceties or the combined status present in the room, faces Douglas down at every turn—including a demand for the nonexistent "Mar-tian national anthem"—and gets him to signify agreement to a document Jubal prepared the night before and presented to his adversary in advance of all the foofaraw. It is a scene worthy of the best of Heinlein's "tall tales," like "The Man Who Sold the Moon."

Black humor and tomfoolery join hands in Mike's visit to the Church of the New Revelation (Fosterite), which bears some resemblance to a commercially resplendent Mormonism. Teenage messengers are "cherubs" with wings who fly by means of "jump harnesses" under their robes. Slot machines give blessings and occasional jackpots—Mike manipulates one to pay off three times in a row for Jubal before Jill stops him—which usually find their way back into the cash registers of the Church. Foster himself has been stuffed and mounted for reverent contemplation, though Mike sees it only as "spoiled food." People are occasionally chosen, like lottery winners, to "go to heaven" with a "Bon Voyage" party and funeral services held the same night, and their estates to go to the Church. And services include snake dances and cheerleaders, glossolalia and bar service, stereovision coverage (the big screen shows football games afterward during the season), with hymns sponsored by approved products, door prizes, subsonic vibrations and other electronic gadgetry in a building designed to shake to the foundations for effect when the congregation claps and stamps its approval.

In presenting this scene, Heinlein goes all out, with foreword and afterword by Jubal, explaining, respectively, that churches can get away with anything, and that this one—he fears—might become totalitarian, because it delivers what it promises: happiness here and now. For all that the satirical lash cuts deeply, Jubal is at pains to explain away the outrageousness, reducing the reader's resistance to the unconventional elements that will later appear in Mike's Church. But Jubal's fear at giving up his individualism is still strong; comparing Fosterism to the Third Reich, Jubal opines that the important consideration is whether the church leader is a scoundrel or a saint. Given the effect of the Fosterites, he hopes Digby is a scoundrel, since "a saint can stir up ten times as much mischief." Since Mike is clearly no scoundrel—though Digby is—this foreshadowing seems to indicate Heinlein's awareness of the dangers inherent in his presentation of this "new" religion based on "Martian" tenets.

Mike's Church of All Worlds is, in a sense, what the whole book has been leading up to, with the piecemeal introduction of its elements going into the making of the Man from Mars. His first "alien" thoughts, which become incorporated into the Church, are of the rituals of cannibalism and water-sharing. For a "people" on a dry world, both practices make eminent sense—why waste food?—but they are also ritual occasions that Jubal salutes as "civilized." Cannibalism is not that rare in human history—a symbolic variety is built into Christian communion—and it recalls myths of human beings partaking of the divine in order to share its strength and immortality (Orpheus, Dionysus, Freud's "primal horde"). In Martian terms, it also symbolizes bodily continuity of the species, while the soul changes state and lives on.

For humans as well as Martians, water is the "essence" of life; though we take it more for granted, we have ceremonies like baptism and uses of "holy" water. "Water-brother" is clearly akin to "blood-brother" as a symbol of friendship, and "sharing water" is like "drinking brotherhood." It leads to "growing together" and perhaps having your eggs "share the same nest." Growing together and "grokking" have a new meaning for Mike when he discovers sex, but sex is hardly a hidden commodity in our culture and the communal fantasy Mike and his associates live out is not new with *Stranger*.

Although sex is divine in its own way, one way to know the God in oneself and others, the real proof is in the parapsychological powers Mike has and teaches others through the medium of the Martian language. Easy to show in fiction, and perhaps only there, these are what convince Jubal that Mike's religion is Truth, as empirical as science. It is hardly a new observation that language conditions culture, but rarely outside science fiction and fantasy is this tenet taken so seriously as to imply that it is only our different upbringing, conditioned by our human languages that prevent us from practicing these "impossible" feats. For the writer, who can make things happen on a piece of paper simply by saying so, this is a beguiling fantasy, one that Heinlein treated early in his career as within reach of all who are trainable in "the discipline," which in this case is learning Martian. Growing together, developing paranormal powers and achieving true wisdom result from knowing how to "grok," or recognizing that one is God, all are God, and the responsibility can not be shirked.

The aim is not so much the achievement of happiness as the alleviation of pain, as is signified by Mike's painful laughter at the plight of the monkeys. Pitying normal man, the church leaders are committed to spreading the "word" or the language as far and fast as possible, at whatever cost to themselves. This desire for wide acceptance, despite the "scandalous" and "blasphemous" activities of Mike's Church, requires a commercial appeal to the populace, aimed primarily at the lower and lower-middle classes, though that is not specified. If Mike has learned anything from Jubal, it is the value of commercialism; capitalizing on popular appeal is a lesson reinforced for Mike by the Fosterites, the carnival, and Las Vegas. Part of the appeal is sexual, part is artistic, and part is the promise, usually frustrated, of happiness. These are united in the person of Patty Paiwonski, whose body is covered with sacred tattoos, and who is like Mike, sexuality and innocence incarnate. Only temporarily is sexuality frustrated in this religion, and innocence is regained, in part because there is no exclusive or possessive commitment; commitment is to the whole of the "water brotherhood" and to potential members of it. But despite the availability of sex, wealth, and happiness to all, they are driven to bring everyone else under the same banner, to validate the worth of their activity.

This messianic zeal and the apparent predestination of who will be among the "elect" cause Slusser to accuse Heinlein of proffering a neo-Calvinist faith in *Stranger*. Indeed, Heinlein has a long history of ambivalence in this regard, dating presumably to his own sense of restriction back home in the Bible Belt. Although he frequently criticizes those who regard themselves as "elect," who restrict the "competent man" from rising to his just reward, and attacks both residual Calvinism in secular societies and the more virulent strain in imagined theocracies, he would set up his own aristocracy or tyranny of the able, of whom Mike is the most extreme example imaginable. Mike is also the judge of who is "elect," whatever the rigamarole of learning the language and the nine circles of initiation; being able to do either is a sign of being elect, and Mike has admitted his earliest "water brothers" without either act, though after the fact they too have taken to learning Martian in quest of their growing together and growing in spirit and powers. Even Jubal gives up sexual abstinence at the end and promises to learn Martian. But for all the resemblances between this and any other body of true believers, Jubal has his reservations, recognizing the problem of responsibility, or whether a "saint" or "scoundrel" is in the driver's seat. Mike clearly is not a scoundrel, so he must be much more dangerous; only an "angel," Jubal maintains, could live up to the responsibility implied by "Thou art God."

On one level of the story, of course, Mike is not just an angel but the Archangel Michael. Patty so identifies him, Digby and Foster confirm the possibility, and after Mike's death, the Archangel puts in an ominous appearance in their comic heaven. But this explanation contradicts the first, making the whole Martian mystique unnecessary. Either these powers are latent in man or neither version deserves any credence, a rather disconcerting denouement for such an elaborate symbolic construct. How else but by angelic judgment, however, can Mike "grok wrongness" in the Secret Service and in a man trying to rob his Church, in Bishop Foster's effigy, and whatever Digby did or said in private after the Fosterite service Mike attended? On the other hand, what kind of punishment for this wrongness is a discorporation that does no irreparable harm, and may send the victim to heaven? Given this kind of logic, or lack of it, the implications seem rather serious of a whole bunch of "water brothers" running around loose with the power and the will to discorporate what wrongly stands in their way. At best, their angelic outlook is different from ours, as is suggested by their cool, almost Martian, appreciation of Mike's final "blowoff," his martyrdom, at which only the skeptical Jubal is moved.

The internal contradictions of the book center on the symbiotic but contradictory relationship between Mike and Jubal, who are both versions of the Heinleinian "competent man." Both are puppet masters, manipulating others as if they had no wills of their own, paying no real attention to anyone except each other. If Jubal is Mike's teacher at the beginning, the roles are soon reversed; since there is not room for two puppet masters in the story, one must give way. The structure of the story dictates that Mike's commitment must win out over Jubal's skepticism, but not without a struggle. The problems of point-of-view and ground level of reality are among the evidences that the fight is incompletely resolved.

The story is about Mike, if we can believe the titles of the five parts, each of which represents a stage in the development of a hero. As a young man, Mike seems to have something in common with the protagonists of Heinlein's juveniles; their characters are in the process of formation, as they learn how to survive in the big world, survival being the prime virtue for a Heinlein hero. Unlike the juvenile heroes, however, Mike does not have to learn how to put up with limitations; superior in every way, he does not so much develop as reveal himself in all his glory. Angel, god, or Martian-educated human, he follows the pattern of the archetypal hero from cradle to grave. He is not so much a character as the story itself; his function is to happen.

If we see him as a person at all, it is as a perpetual innocent, despite Jubal's assurances to Duke that Mike is really more civilized than anyone else. He is untouched by his learning, except that he discovers better how to cope; he does not form his character by compromise as Heinlein's earlier adolescent heroes did. Sex and pity do not corrupt his innocence, as neither involves his really interacting with anyone else; in fact, his disciples either are, or become, equally innocent, or holy. Perhaps only innocents could live up to the angelic commitment of their faith, a commitment that in Mike's case will lead not to survival in the usual sense, but rather to martyrdom. Heinlein undercuts that ending, of course, but at a cost; Jubal must become apostle to the risen god, after playing Thomas to Mike's Messiah.

This is an ill-fitting role for Jubal to play, not only in the context of the book, but also in the niche Jubal occupies among Heinlein's creations. Where Mike departs from the patterns of the "first-stage" Heinlein hero, Jubal is typical of the "third-stage," the garrulous old man who has seen every-thing and is now best suited to relating it to anyone who will listen (the terms are Panshin's). He has already proved him-self at the "second stage" in several careers, three of which he still carries on. Having seen claims exploded, he is pre-dominantly skeptical and uncommitted, pragmatic about what works but amoral about the values he knows so well how to manipulate. A manipulator of people as well, he is only slightly more respectful of them, and never awed, except for his conversion to faith in Mike.

But there is another side to Jubal as well, some of which is coincident with this characterization, some of which comes out mainly in his apostolic function late in the book. Skeptical, he does not necessarily reject commitment as a matter of principle. He seems to revel in his own contradictions, but he is also world-weary. As an intellectual in a society he can manipulate, he is to some extent a victim of *anomie:* rootless, lacking social norms and values. Jill calls him cynical, which implies a disillusioned idealism; he wants to believe in some-thing, but can't.

When Mike gives him something to believe in, Truth, which his senses can not deny, Jubal capitulates, but he resists all the way. Although he grudgingly accepts the evidence of his Fair Witness and a set of movie cameras when Mike plays around with inanimate objects, Jubal doesn't want to know the facts when Mike discorporates the police. Again, he refuses the knowledge that Mike has done away with Digby, so as not to be an accessory. Hearing reports about Mike from a distance, he gradually comes to believe that the boy can do anything. He even defends Mike's Church to Ben Caxton, though he refuses to join it, or even to visit Mike until the Church burns down. Then he requires seducing by Dawn, Mike's discorporation, and being saved from a stroke to be finally won over.

Jubal's changeability is also evident in his opinions, of which there are a myriad. This aspect of his character is the primary vehicle of Heinlein's satire, but in a number of cases, the satirist is inconsistent, either recanting what he said earlier, or acting contrary to an expressed belief. Though he's too old for sex and the performance is monotonous, he still checks out pornography sent to Mike, before turning it over to Duke, and eventually is reborn through his encounter with Dawn; a firm believer in sexual privacy, he (unknowingly) shares this experience with everyone in Mike's nest. Jubal sees organized religions as the enemy of freedom, individualism, even sanity, yet he sees their logical function as producing happiness and becomes Mike's apostle, writing the first gospel of His incarnation. Politics for Jubal means not compromise but exploitation on the large scale (the Federation) and the small (his own household). But from chief manipulator—on behalf of Mike's interest—he becomes himself the victim of Mike's manipulations, because of his interest in Mike.

Jubal's views on art may be of special value here. In his showdown with Douglas and again in the Fosterite Tabernacle, he sees music as exploitative. His taste in visual art is "literary," geared to the story it tells as in "The Little Mermaid" and Rodin's "Caryatid Who Has Fallen Under Her Stone," both of which symbolize to him Mike, or man in Mike's scheme of things. Discussing this with Ben, Jubal launches into an attack on the abstractions of modern art, which, since they don't communicate with the general public, are "pseudo-intellectual masturbation," unlike real "creative art," which is "intercourse, in which the artist renders emotional his audience." The sexual metaphor is intriguing, given the nature of Mike's religion, but Jubal is in full flight now, shifting to the art of writing:

> "Artist" is a word I avoid for the same reason I hate to be called "Doctor." But I *am* an artist. Most of my stuff is worth reading only once . . . and not even once by a person who

knows the little I have to say. But I am an *honest* artist. What
I write is intended to reach the customer—and affect him, if
possible with pity and terror . . . or at least divert the tedium
of his hours. I *never* hide from him in a private language, nor
am I seeking praise from other writers for "technique" or
other balderdash. I want praise from the customer, given in
cash because I've reached him—or I don't want anything."
[Italics and ellipses in original.]

In this exercise in applied Aristotle, Jubal expresses himself
in terms similar to those Heinlein has used to describe his
own writing. Besides having application to how he wants this
book read, this passage calls explicit attention to that identi-
fication with Jubal that he resents, suggesting there may be a
"private language" at work here of which he is relatively unaware.

Jubal is parallel to Heinlein not only in profession, his
avowed commercialism, but also in some of his opinions and
their inconsistency, in his individualism and general crotcheti-
ness, in his all-around experience and competence, even in age
(i.e., Jubal must have been born around 1907 to be his apparent age around the turn of the next century). And Jubal
is the major viewpoint character of the book, not acting so
much as reacting, primarily to the Man from Mars. His consistency, such as it is, is all we have to go on, inside the book, in
judging or evaluating Mike and his behavior. What Mike does,
Jubal explains, rationalizing away his own rationality at times.
Thus he acts as a surrogate for the reader. If this skeptic can
become a believer, this individualist can become part of a self-
effacing movement, this critic of man's folly can learn to love
his neighbor, how long can we be expected to hold out, at least
on a first, perhaps hurried reading ("most of my stuff is worth
reading only once")?

Jubal is a surrogate for both the reader and the writer.
Like Ben and Jill, he performs multiple functions, contradictory perhaps, but economical. In the first half of the book, he
is Mike's mentor, the traditional advisor who appears in hero
myths, as in Heinlein's own novels. In the second half, however, the teacher becomes the pupil, "the child is father to the

man." Having done his part to create Mike, he is taken over by his own creation. Although there is also an omniscient narrator, only vaguely realized, Jubal is the real teller of the tale implicitly, even before he begins to dictate his version. As the archetypal hero, Mike is the story, he is what happens. But Jubal is who it happens to, the man who has to tell it, even if he doesn't believe it. Just as Heinlein apparently stumbled onto the hero archetype with Mike, whose story exceeds Heinlein's normal limits, so in Jubal he may have reinvented the "artist as epic hero," as W. H. Auden describes the Romantic author. Nostalgic for innocence, but dedicated to the "exploration of the hitherto unknown and unconscious," especially within himself, the Romantic writer celebrated his own greatness in his characters:

> Faust, Don Juan, Captain Ahab are not really the heroes of their respective books, but the imaginative projections of their creators, i.e., what they do is not really done as a man of action acts for the sake of the act, but in order to know what it feels like to act. Ahab is, so to speak, what it feels like to be Ishmael the recorder. The artist who has thus to be at once the subject of his experiment and the recorder enjoys excitement and suffers terrors hardly known before.

Given the air of rationality that Jubal, like Heinlein, pretends to, and the appropriation of narrative forms associated with the pre-Romantic Age of Enlightenment, it may seem odd to group the author of *Stranger* with the Romantic poets, excited with and terrified by their own temerity. But this kind of self-consciousness has been continuous since the Romantic period, visible for example in the *Doppelgänger* figure of late nineteenth-century fiction and the high proportion of autobiographical novels in the twentieth century. A parallel case is Robert Penn Warren's *All the King's Men* (1946), a superior example of the species, in which the protagonist, Willie Stark, is "what it feels like to be" Jack Burden, the fascinated narrator.

Charting Heinlein's self-consciousness has been the thankless, self-appointed task of Alexei Panshin, who is convinced that underneath the extroverted, commercial exterior there is indeed an excited and terrified interior man. For Panshin, the key to the real Heinlein, the "private language" as it were, is the author's fascination with solipsism, the belief that no one, perhaps nothing, exists except oneself, that all is illusion produced by one's imagination. It is an aberration perhaps especially suited to the writer of fantasy, and one that is charged with excitement, even terror, in three short stories: "They," which posits the truth of that belief when the manipulators are seen making the illusions; "By His Bootstraps," in which time travel enables a hero to educate himself and to fear change; and "All You Zombies," in which the protagonist turns out to be his/her own father and mother. But solipsism is implicit in all those stories in which an older Heinlein surrogate teaches a younger one how to cope, in the role playing of *Double Star,* the manipulating parasites of *The Puppet Masters,* the time-traveling fairy tale of *The Door into Summer* (all in the Fifties), not to mention the elaborate self-creations of *I Will Fear No Evil* and *Time Enough for Love.* It is perhaps most explicit, outside the short stories, in *Beyond This Horizon* (1941), when a disembodied consciousness samples several characters before voluntarily limiting itself to the viewpoint of the awakening Hamilton Felix, for whom survival *after death* is the prime question.

In *Stranger in a Strange Land,* solipsism is implicit in the manipulations of Mike and Jubal, especially in Mike's mental power over inanimate and animate matter. On the Martian plane, it is suggested or paralleled by the adult Martians' control of plants, by their cannibalistic rituals (like the snake devouring its own tail) and by their continuity with the Old Ones. More explicitly, Patty Paiwonski and "Alice" Douglas are both identified in heaven as "holy temporals" assigned to earthside duty, limited to individual human consciousnesses. And the Archangel Michael is identified as "one of the most eager Solipsism players in this sector." Even Jubal in a wry moment claims, once every leap year, to regard Creation as a matter of "sheer solipsist debauchery"; the rest of the time, if he thinks of it at all, he alternates between a "created" and a "noncreated" universe.

The true solipsist of the piece, however, is Heinlein himself, like any author willing his creations into existence. For all his claims, in various places, to want people to live by "the scientific method," his imagined societies work—on paper, despite the carpings of critics—because he wills them to. According to the dust jacket of *Stranger,* his admittedly unreachable "purpose in writing this novel was to examine every major axiom of Western culture, to question every axiom, throw doubt on it—and, if possible—to make the antithesis of each axiom appear a possible and perhaps a desirable thing —rather than unthinkable." This grandiose scheme seems conceivable only to an author who takes it for granted that he can create the real and unreal alike, and make his audience sit still for it. Like Jubal, he may be "fooling around," but for serious purposes.

One of them—as Panshin insists—is a concern for what life is worth living for; why else would he throw in all those passages in which Jubal opines about creation, life and death, art and religion? Heinlein's perennial answer is survival for its own sake; thus Jubal, like Lazarus Long in *Methuselah's Children* and *Time Enough for Love,* seems destined to live forever. But Jubal is also a creator—of commercial art, and of Mike, who repays the compliment by calling him "father," making him a "patron saint," and waiting for his blessing before he accepts his martyrdom. As a creator—the original solipsist—Jubal/Heinlein knows that none of this exists except in his imagination, but his creation is troublesome. Mike is invincibly innocent, as Jubal/Heinlein is not, though he may have nostalgic longings for that state. His creation nourishes him—literally in the story, as a broth—forcing him to feed off himself. If Jubal is a mirror, as he tells Ben, in which Mike sees what he wants to see, Mike is the same, for Jubal/Heinlein and for many readers. Mike, however, has the Martian sense of appreciating life as a rounded whole; he seems to know what life is worth living—and dying—for. Jubal recoils from this until he senses or imagines Mike's presence in his bedroom; then, he is free to write his gospel, accepting the form Mike's life has taken.

The book's confusion, then, stems in part from the contradiction between an exemplary tale of men like gods and a solipsistic sense that it's all make-believe. The sophisticated reader may see this as confusion, rejecting both fantasies as adolescent wish-fulfillment. But the more naive audience might more easily accept what it wants to, from the satirical denigration of common knowledge and established tradition to the assumption of godlike powers. The audience in the Sixties, I suspect, has the latter reaction. Aside from the traditional science fiction subculture, Heinlein's readers were young, relatively untutored in literary analysis, certainly not schooled in literary readings of science fiction. College students, and other members of the "counterculture" that grew in the wake of the loss of John Kennedy's dream of Camelot, and in shared opposition to a technocratic society that had no use for them except as cannon fodder, devoured *Stranger in a Strange Land* and handed it on. Its reputation grew by word of mouth, as a "book of wisdom" for our time, an "underground classic."

Heinlein was regarded as a sage, a guru, unafraid to give direction, when more conventional teachers feared to advocate anything but tolerance. The example of Valentine Michael Smith could be invoked by Jesus people, by sexual revolutionaries, and by political radicals, all of whom rejected the existing order and wanted to impose their own, admittedly very fuzzy, ideas of utopia on an uncomprehending middle-class society, simply trying to cope with everyday existence. Some went so far as to establish cults of "water-brotherhood," to view "Father Jubal" Heinlein as indeed a "patron saint," and to find further indications in his later "sacred texts" of his commitment to their cause. Others, like the Manson "family," tried to live Mike's sexual utopia and to discorporate their imagined enemies, who in this life were not so easily assured of immortality in a comic heaven.

Criticism of the book for bad taste in style or contents

would hardly have been welcome, except as evidence of the critic's defense of the Establishment. Besides, old-fashioned ideas of taste were part of what the book attacked. In addition, it offered, with impenetrably confusing irony, a new program to establish utopia on Earth in which everyone who believed would love and share. It even seemed to be preaching revolution, at the cost of martyrdom if necessary. And the decade bore these supposed teachings out, in abortive form, from the Flower Children to the Weathermen. Even the most "shocking" aspects of *Stranger* seem pale against the background of the last seventeen years, and its solipsism fits right in to today's "laid-back" hedonism, in which everyone is trying to find—or create—the "real me."

As the book's popularity grew throughout the decade, Heinlein would have been a fool not to see where the growing audience was. The three novels he wrote during this period were more conventional, though studded with social commentary. But by the Seventies the lesson took hold and his most recent books, disliked intensely in the science fiction community but snapped up by the public at large, are primarily novels of sex and opinions. The world as it is they virtually condemn out of hand, while they indulge in wish-fulfillment fantasies with hardly a glance back at plausibility.

The rest of the science fiction community—not to mention Hollywood—were not slow to catch on, either. "Science fiction" became a major growth industry in paperbacks, movies, and television shows with superheroes and paranormal powers, sexual titillation, and slapdash construction. Technology and mysticism have always been at war in science fiction, but Heinlein helped tip the balance away from the former toward the latter. The biggest individual sellers may be—it's debatable—examples of "hard" science fiction, or books by authors noted for it. The vast majority of "science fiction" marketed in the seventies, however, seems totally divorced from any real world of scientific, technological, social, and psychological limits. The best-selling paperback series, in fact, claiming at least blood kinship with science fiction, is the Gor volumes by John Norman, outright sword-and-sorcery, reeking with sex and sadism.

Heinlein did not create that market, any more than he created Charles Manson. But he was among the first in the postwar era to exploit it, and to confirm his reputation, if not as a forger of new trails, at least as a barometer of public taste. An intensely personal book, *Stranger in a Strange Land* also implied a great deal about the state of society, past and future, in spite of its dearth of futuristic trappings. The makings of a significant work of art may be buried in it, in a welter of story and symbol and correspondences between art and sex and religion. But a better book might have defeated its purpose. The problem of what to do with one's life was at the root of the Sixties' social unrest, just as it is today in the "Me" Decade. A better book would not have spoken to that ferment in the same way, and could never have had as great an effect.

Notes

PAGE	QUOTE	SOURCE

1. Asimov's Robots (Fiedler and Mele)

1	"If, in future"	Isaac Asimov, *The Rest of the Robots* (Garden City, N.Y.: Doubleday, 1964), p. 43.
2	"machines designed by"	Ibid., p. xiii.
2	Three Laws	Asimov, *I, Robot* (Garden City, N.Y.: Doubleday, 1963), p. 51. [The first edition of *I, Robot,* published by Gnome Press in 1950, is out of print.]
4	"brains of platinum"	*The Rest of the Robots*, p. 42.
7	"no Machine may"	*I, Robot*, p. 216.
7	"It was always"	Ibid., p. 218.
7	"For all time"	Ibid.
9	"no more than"	*The Rest of the Robots*, p. 86.
10	"Robots have no"	Ibid., pp. 108–9.
11	"For two hundred"	Ibid., pp.161–62.
11	"three or four"	Ibid., p. 165.
12	"Each City"	Ibid., p. 181.
13	"There were the"	Ibid., pp. 177–78.
15	"What are we"	Ibid., pp. 326–27.
17	"He had an"	Ibid., p. 377.
17	"An observer from"	Ibid., p. 384.
19	"Solaria inside out"	Ibid., p. 551.
20	"courage to face"	Ibid., pp. 550–51.
20	"had left the"	Ibid., p. 553.
20	"While I was"	Ibid., p. 555.

2. The Invasion Stories of Ray Bradbury (Johnson)

23	"What's the name"	Ray Bradbury, "Zero Hour," in *The Illustrated Man* (New York: Bantam, 1952), p. 169.
23	H. G. Wells	*The War of the Worlds* and *The Invisible Man* are available in one volume, with an introduction by Arthur C. Clarke, from Pocket Books, New York.
24	*War of the Worlds* broadcast	The complete script of Orson Welles's radio adaptation of *The War of the Worlds,* plus newspaper clippings and historical notes relating to the broadcast, may be found in Howard Koch, *The Panic Broadcast* (New York: Avon, 1971).
24	"The Fog Horn"	Bradbury, "The Fog Horn," in *The Golden Apples of the Sun* (New York: Bantam, 1961).

PAGE	QUOTE	SOURCE
24	*The Beast from 20,000 Fathoms*	*The Beast from 20,000 Fathoms* appears on late-night television from time to time. The film is remembered chiefly for the special effects—especially the three-dimensional animation—by Ray Harryhausen. Details about the making of the film may be found in *From the Land Beyond* by Jeff Rovin (New York: Berkley Windhover, 1977).
25	"They're so snooty"	Bradbury, "Zero Hour," in *The Illustrated Man*, p. 173.
25	"Drill says you're"	Ibid.
25	"Peekaboo"	Ibid., p. 177.
26	"What would you say"	Bradbury, "Boys! Raise Giant Mushrooms in *Your* Cellar!", in *The Machineries of Joy* (New York: Bantam, 1965), p. 47.
26	"Maybe there's something wrong"	Ibid., p. 50.
27	"He looked back"	Ibid., p. 62.
28	"My hand"	Bradbury, "Fever Dream," in *A Medicine for Melancholy* (New York: Bantam, 1960), p. 52.
28	"At four o'clock"	Ibid.
28	"What would happen"	Ibid., p. 54.
29	"his brain fill"	Ibid., p. 56.
30	"Evil has only"	Bradbury, *Something Wicked This Way Comes* (New York: Bantam, 1963), p. 204.
31	"Sometimes I actually"	Bradbury, "Let's Play Poison," originally in *Dark Carnival*. *Dark Carnival* is now out of print. The quote is taken from the story as reprinted in *The Small Assassin*, a British paperback published by Panther Books, Ltd., Frogmore, St. Albans, Herts, and available in some larger U.S. bookstores.
31	"The wails of a lifetime"	Ibid., p. 36.
32	"evil for no reason"	Bradbury, "Perhaps We Are Going Away," in *The Machineries of Joy*, p. 71.
32	"They scanned the prairies"	Ibid., p. 72.
32	"I feel them pass"	Ibid.
32	"Not you or me"	Ibid., p. 73.
32	"a great dark canoe"	Ibid.
33	"She walks in beauty"	(Lord Byron), in Bradbury, "The Summer Night," in *The Martian Chronicles* (New York: Bantam, 1951), p. 15.
33	"as delicate as"	Ibid., p. 14.

PAGE	QUOTE	SOURCE
34	"I live in a well"	Bradbury, "The One Who Waits," in *The Machineries of Joy*, p. 14.
34	"Now I know who I am"	Ibid., p. 15.
35	"I hear . . . a voice"	Ibid., p. 17.
35	"When the first rocket"	Bradbury, "Ylla," in *The Martian Chronicles*, p. 2.
35	"Another expedition"	Bradbury, "The Third Expedition," ibid., p. 32.
36	"Look here"	Bradbury, "The Off Season," ibid., p. 134.
37	"He felt submerged"	Bradbury, "Dark They Were, and Golden-Eyed," in *A Medicine for Melancholy*, p. 94.
38	" 'Sam,' Bitterling said"	Ibid., p. 100.
38	"Such odd, ridiculous"	Ibid., p. 107.
39	"Who ever heard"	Bradbury, "The Concrete Mixer," in *The Illustrated Man*, p. 140.

3. From Concept to Fable (O'Reilly)

42	"It began with a concept"	A brief reminiscence written by Frank Herbert for jacket copy of *Dune: The Banquet Scene, Read by the Author* (New York: Caedmon Records, 1977).
43	"I had far too much"	An unpublished interview with Frank and Beverly Herbert by Willis McNelly, Fairfax, California, February 3, 1969.
44	"the primitives of the Kalahari"	Ibid.
44	"It is vital"	Herbert, *Dune* (New York: Berkley Publishing Co., 1965), p. 507.
45	"a new 'avatar' "	Unpublished interview by McNelly.
45	"It might become a new"	Jacket copy, *Dune: The Banquet Scene*.
46	"an 'aristocratic bureaucracy' "	Ibid.
46	"Feudalism is a natural"	Unpublished interview by McNelly.
46	"You gain insights"	Jacket copy, *Dune: The Banquet Scene*.
47	"Hawat started to leap"	*Dune*, pp. 155–56.
51	"He sampled the time winds"	Ibid., p. 482.
53	"The stories that"	Unpublished interview by McNelly.
54	"I wanted a sense"	Unpublished interview with Herbert by Timothy O'Reilly, New York City, February 27, 1978.
54	"the sound of a passage"	Unpublished interview by O'Reilly.
55	"It's a coital rhythm"	Unpublished interview by McNelly.
55	"the function of science-fiction"	Herbert, "Science Fiction and a World in Crisis," in *Science Fiction: Today and Tomorrow*, ed. Reginald

PAGE	QUOTE	SOURCE

		Bretnor (Baltimore, Md.: Penguin Books, 1974), p. 71.
55	"a 'training manual' "	Unpublished interview by O'Reilly.

4. Androgynes in Outer Space (Bucknall)

56	All references to Le Guin's article on *The Left Hand of Darkness*	Ursula Le Guin, "Is Gender Necessary?" in *Aurora: Beyond Equality*, ed. Vonda N. McIntyre and Susan Janice Anderson (Greenwich, Conn.: Fawcett Publications, 1976).
59	"*Light is the left hand*"	Le Guin, *The Left Hand of Darkness* (New York: Ace Books, 1976), p. 267.
61	"This seemed to put"	Ibid., p. 61.
61	"Praise then darkness"	From the Handdara grace of invocation, "Praise then Darkness and Creation unfinished," ibid., p. 246.
63	"Karhide is not a nation"	Ibid., p. 6.
65	"in the Sight"	Ibid., p. 164.
65	"*Light is the left hand*"	Ibid., pp. 233–34.
67	"desire and pursuit"	A passage in Plato's *Symposium*, in which Aristophanes, discussing the Androgyne, says that what lovers most desire is to become one person: "The reason is that this was our primitive condition when we were wholes, and love is simply the name for the desire and pursuit of the whole." Plato, *The Symposium* (London: Penguin Books, 1951), p. 64.

5. Sisters, Daughters, and Aliens (Podojil)

73	"Martha begat"	Judith Merril, "Daughters of Earth," in *The Best of Judith Merril* (New York: Warner Books, 1976), p. 75.
73	"There are such similarities"	Ibid., p. 137.
73	"Perhaps the others"	Ibid., p. 138.
74	"it had been firmly"	Ibid., p. 90.
75	"Military virtues"	Le Guin, American SF and the Other, in *Science Fiction Studies*, #7, Vol. 2, Part 3 (November, 1975).
77	"We each have a book"	James Tiptree, Jr., "Houston, Houston, Do You Read?" in *Star Songs of an Old Primate* (New York: Ballantine Books, 1968), p. 208.
78	"What kind of songs"	Ibid., p. 210.
78	"Nothing but"	Ibid., p. 217.
79	"We're trying"	Ibid., p. 224.
79	"Your problem is"	Ibid., p. 225.
81	"Oh, there wasn't"	James Tiptree, Jr., "The Women Men

PAGE	QUOTE	SOURCE
		Don't See," in *Warm Worlds and Otherwise* (New York: Ballantine Books, 1975), p. 152.
81	"Men hate wars"	Ibid., p. 154.
81	"go sight unseen"	Ibid., p. 163.
81	"A great tragedy"	Joanna Russ, "When It Changed," in *The New Women of Wonder*, ed. Pamela Sargeant (New York: Vintage Books, 1977), p. 232.
82	"Yuki, do you think"	Ibid., p. 238.
83	"This is how"	Sondra Dorman, "Building Block," ibid., p. 296.

SELECTED BIBLIOGRAPHY

McIntyre, Vonda N., and Susan Janice Anderson, eds. *Aurora: Beyond Equality*. Greenwich, Connecticut, Fawcett, 1976. Includes "Houston, Houston, Do You Read?"

Merril, Judith. *The Best of Judith Merril*. New York: Warner Books, 1976. Includes *Daughters of Earth*.

Russ, Joanna. *Picnic on Paradise*. London: W. H. Allen & Co., Ltd., 1976.

——— *We Who Are About To. . . .* New York: Dell, 1977.

Sargeant, Pamela, ed. *Women of Wonder: Science Fiction Stories by Women about Women*. New York: Vintage, 1975.

——— *More Women of Wonder: Science Fiction Novelettes by Women about Women*. New York: Vintage, 1976.

——— *The New Women of Wonder: Recent Science Fiction Stories by Women about Women*. New York: Vintage, 1977. Includes "The Women Men Don't See," "When It Changed," and "Building Block." Other works by Russ and Dorman are in the first two volumes.

Tiptree, James, Jr. *Star Songs of an Old Primate*. New York: Ballantine/Del Ray, 1978. Includes "Houston, Houston, Do You Read?"

——— *Ten Thousand Light Years from Home*. New York: Ace, 1973.

——— *Warm Worlds and Otherwise*. New York: Ballantine, 1975. Includes "The Women Men Don't See."

6. The Appeal of *Childhood's End* (Menger)

88	"An end that repudiated optimism"	Arthur C. Clarke, *Childhood's End* (New York: Ballantine Books, 1953), p. 201.
90	"huge and silent"	Ibid., p. 5.
91	"Only one thought"	Ibid.
92	"overwhelming intellectual power"	Ibid., p. 14.

PAGE	QUOTE	SOURCE
92	"mastery of the physical universe"	Ibid., p. 213.
??	"Surely you'd study"	Ibid., p. 83.
93	"I never believed"	Ibid., p. 170.
94	"I never believed in the supernatural"	Ibid., p. 171.
94	"I will not deceive"	Ibid., p. 172.
??	"I cannot explain"	Ibid., p. 179.
95	"All these potentialities"	Ibid.
96	"There were drawbacks"	Ibid., p. 107.
96	"In this galaxy of ours"	Ibid., p. 132.
97	"They would hold fast"	Ibid., p. 214.
98	"Though it might be"	Ibid., p. 60.
98	"Really, darling!"	Ibid., p. 81.
100	"It was an impossible"	Ibid., p. 106.
100	"What finally decided"	Ibid., p. 118.
101	"And the children"	Ibid., p. 140.
101	"And for the first time"	Ibid., p. 4.
101	"he had never thought"	Ibid., p. 34.
102	"overgrown baby"	Ibid., p. 34.
102	"Would you take"	Ibid., p. 117.
103	"This was the moment"	Ibid., p. 5.
104	"When the Overlords"	Ibid., p. 89, 71, 144.
105	"The ship's prow"	Ibid., p. 1.
106	"The human race continued"	Ibid., p. 107.
106	"For a lifetime, mankind"	Ibid., p. 133.
106	"High above, a meteor"	Ibid., p. 24.
106	"It was the wall of a siren"	Ibid., p. 150.
106	"He clasped his arms"	Ibid., p. 185.
107	"A great red sun"	Ibid., p. 168.
107	"Six colored suns"	Ibid., p. 169.

7. A World of Difference (von Glahn)

111	"That's a whole lot"	Samuel R. Delany, *The Einstein Intersection* (New York: Ace Books, 1967), pp. 5–6.
112	"to any functional"	Ibid., p. 9.
114	"Back outside this morning"	Ibid., p. 78.
114	"the mythical form"	Ernst Cassirer, *Language and Myth*, trans. Suzanne K. Langer (New York: Dover Publications, 1946), p. 33.
115	"I can remember"	*The Einstein Intersection*, p. 39.
117	"I remember a year"	Ibid., p. 118.
120	"When what I saw"	Ibid., p. 63.
122	"I can hand you"	Ibid., p. 103.
122	"Anyway, Green-eye"	Ibid., p. 93.
123	"Kid Death can control"	Ibid., p. 133.
123	"He needs patterning"	Ibid.
123	"The past terrifies me"	Ibid., p. 86.

PAGE	QUOTE	SOURCE
125	"In any closed mathematical"	Ibid., p. 128.
126	"I don't want to know"	Ibid., p. 130.
127	"The world is not"	Ibid., p. 131.
127	"Do you want to see"	Ibid., p. 146.
128	"Like the Kid"	Ibid., p. 154.
129	"Jean Harlow?"	Ibid., p. 107.
129	"The floor began"	Ibid., p. 148.
130	"It's still the wrong"	Ibid.

For a more systematic discussion of the mythology, see Stephen Scobie, "Different Mazes: Mythology in Samuel R. Delany's 'The Einstein Intersection,'" in *Riverside Quarterly* 5 (1971): 12–18.

8. An Ideal of Three (Sackmary)

132	"Shore Leave"	A script by Theodore Sturgeon for the December 29, 1966 episode of the television show *Star Trek*. Listed in David Gerrold, *The World of Star Trek* (New York: Ballantine Books, 1973), p. 131. (Gerrold writes: "I believe *Star Trek* to be one of the finest television formats ever conceived. It proved this with episodes like "City on the Edge of Forever," "Errand of Mercy," "Shore Leave," and "Charlie X." Ibid., p. 260.)
134	*Visuddhi-Magga*	Buddhaghosa, *Visuddhi-Magga*, ed. C. A. F. Rhys-Davids (London: Polytext Society, H. Milford Pub., 1920–21), 1: 77.
136	"It was a modal"	Sturgeon, "Rule of Three," in *Galaxy Reader of Science Fiction*, ed. H. L. Gold (New York: Crown Publishers, 1952), pp. 65, 67.
136	"as if a curtain"	Ibid., p. 68.
137	"when you gave me your heart"	Sturgeon, "Thunder and Roses," in John W. Campbell, Jr., ed., *The Astounding Science Fiction Anthology* (New York: Simon & Schuster, 1951), p. 358.
137	"Extrapolation"	*Sturgeon in Orbit* (New York: Jove/HBJ, 1978), pp. 9–35. (Originally published as *Beware the Fury* [New York: Ziff-Davis Publishing Co., 1953].)
139	Alvin Toffler	Alvin Toffler, *Future Shock* (New York: Random House, 1970).
139	"The firebird's wing"	Sturgeon, "The Touch of Your Hand," in *A Touch of Strange* (New York: DAW Books, 1978), p. 35. (Originally

PAGE	QUOTE	SOURCE
		published 1953 by Galaxy Publishing Corp.)
140	"Twink"	Sturgeon, *Caviar* (New York: Ballantine, 1977), pp. 163–182. (Originally published in *Galaxy Science Fiction*, 1955.)
141	"So nobody wants you"	Sturgeon, *More Than Human* (New York: Ballantine, 1976), p. 183. Other important tales that follow the model described in the article include "Make Room for Me," "The Wages of Synergy," "Hurricane Trio," and "The Sex Opposite"; these four utilize alien forces much the way it occurs in "Rule of Three."

9. *Stranger* in the Sixties (Samuelson)

PAGE	QUOTE	SOURCE
146	"the Manson family"	Vincent Bugliosi, with Curt Gentry, *Helter Skelter: The True Story of the Manson Murders* (New York: Bantam Books, 1976), pp. 321–30; and Ed Sanders, *The Family: The Story of Charles Manson's Dune Buggy Attack Battalion* (New York: Avon Books, 1972), pp. 32–36, 386.
156	Alexei Panshin	Alexei Panshin, *Heinlein in Dimension* (Chicago: Advent, 1968), p. 98.
158	Robert Plank	Robert Plank, "Omnipotent Cannibals: Thoughts on Reading Heinlein's 'Stranger in a Strange Land,'" *Riverside Quarterly* 5 (July, 1971) pp. 30–37.
158	"at any time"	*Heinlein in Dimension*, p. 102.
160	Panshin	Alexei and Cory Panshin, *SF in Dimension: A Book of Explorations* (Chicago: Advent, 1976), pp. 93–195.
162	"a saint can stir up"	Robert A. Heinlein, *Stranger in A Strange Land* (New York: Putnam, 1961), Science Fiction Book Club edition, p. 243.
164	Slusser	George Edward Slusser, *Robert A. Heinlein: Stranger in His Own Land* (San Bernardino, Calif.: Borgo Press, 1976), p. 27.
167	"stages of" Heinlein hero	*Heinlein in Dimension*, pp. 169–172.
168	"pseudo-intellectual masturbation"	*Stranger in A Strange Land*, p. 305.
168	" 'Artist' is a word"	Ibid., p. 306.
170	"Faust, Don Juan"	W. H. Auden, *The Enchafed Flood, or The Romantic Iconography of the Sea* (New York: Vintage, 1967), pp. 147–48.

About the Contributors

BARBARA J. BUCKNALL teaches French at Brock University in Ontario, Canada. She has degrees from Oxford and from Northwestern University and has published extensively on Proust.

JEAN FIEDLER has published a number of novels, stories, and children's stories, along with articles and filmstrips. She is also a teacher and freelance editor.

WAYNE JOHNSON is an editor, freelance writer, and reviewer.

LUCY MENGER is a writer and market researcher. This is her first essay in the field of science fiction.

TIM O'REILLY is a freelance writer, reviewer, and translator.

JIM MELE is editor of *Cross Country* magazine, a journalist, and a poet.

CATHERINE PODOJIL is a freelance writer and reviewer with a particular interest in feminist literature and culture.

REGINA SACKMARY is assistant professor of English at Queensborough Community College, New York City, and a freelance editor and reviewer.

DAVID N. SAMUELSON, professor of English at California State University at Long Beach, is the author of *Visions of Tomorrow*, a book-length study of the science fiction novel, and numerous articles and reviews on science fiction.

GEORGE A. VON GLAHN has taught at the University of Missouri—St. Louis and is the author of articles on science fiction and related fields in the *Encyclopedia of World Literature in the Twentieth Century*. He was recently ordained a minister in the Episcopal Church.